Where Duty Calls

Building Bridges of Hope over 130 Years

Don Axcell

To the Guardian of our souls

and

the men and women who guard our streets

Contents

Contents

Acknowledgements

I would like to acknowledge my grateful thanks to the many people who have made the publication of this book a reality. Without their active assistance it would not have seen the light of day.

Firstly, my thanks to the Trustees of the Christian Police Association for their encouragement and for the access I was afforded to much archive material, including just about every copy of the magazine *On and Off Duty* since 1883. I think that I turned almost every page. I must also thank the staff of the Angus Library and Archive at Regents Park College, Oxford for facilitating my access to the writings of the Gurney family, from which I gained much historical background.

I would heartily pay tribute to those who have helped bring my mountain of scrawling to its published form. To my daughter, Alison Dean, for the hours she has willingly spent listening to my voice and typing out firstly my research notes and then my prose. To my wife, Eleanor, for her dedicated hours of proofreading and constant encouragement. For the expertise and detailed work of my editor, Sheila Jacobs and the design and publishing assistance of SpiffingCovers.

Finally, I would like to give my heartfelt thanks to all my family and friends who have encouraged, prodded and helped me each step of the way over the last seven years to bring this project to completion.

Foreword

It is truly amazing! From a small beginning with a small lady in the late nineteenth century when Catherine Gurney responded to a seemingly insignificant response of an officer ('Do you think a policeman has a soul?'), that the vast organisation – the Christian Police Association – has developed. Until now, its history has remained with the members, past and present, largely unrecorded except for snippets in the publication *On and Off Duty*.

So it is with much gratitude that Don Axcell has – in addition to his daily task as Executive Director – delved into the past long before the Association was born and from documentation, magazine articles, minute-books and other authorities produced this complete history of the Association.

Of course, the organisation will continue and further history will be added but, no doubt, a second volume will be produced in another century. For now, it is evident that this vibrant, international, corporate testimony and fellowship of Christian police officers in all ranks is, under the mighty hand of God our Father, a strong and deeply positive witness both to colleagues and the public to whom we give service.

Robin Oake
KStJ MBE QPM LLB FCMI

Introduction

It has been said that 'Policing is one of the noblest professions. The actions of a police officer, in an instant, can impact an individual for life and even a community for generations' (Dr Stephen Covey).[1] It is also true that those same actions can produce life-changing injuries, mental trauma and family breakdown in the lives of those who put on the uniform and pledge themselves to observe and uphold the law of the land.

While police officers are called upon night and day, 365 days a year, to respond to the calls of the public, who cares for their needs? This is no new phenomenon. For as long as there has been an organised Police Service this question has arisen, but thankfully there have been those who have responded positively. One such person was Catherine Gurney, born in the mid-nineteenth century in a suburb of London. Police officers across the United Kingdom and beyond have much to thank her for. They will remember her for a variety of reasons even though they never met her. Many will not know anything of her background, her work or her legacy, but they will none the less be thankful.

I first heard about Catherine Gurney while training to be a police officer. As far as I knew at that time, her only work was in founding the Christian Police Association, but as I learned more about her I discovered a remarkable woman, driven by her Christian faith to have a passionate concern for the spiritual and physical welfare of police officers.

There is always a danger in writing about historical events that they end up just being a string of date-related occurrences, but I hope that you will see beyond that and capture an appreciation of what she was able to achieve over a period of some fifty years. The five charitable works that she initiated are still in operation today. The convalescent homes she started for police officers have morphed into rehabilitation centres. The concerns she had over the children of officers who died in service or were medically retired are still catered for today. The desire for police officers to acknowledge the spiritual side of their being is still there in the twenty-first century.

While my primary aim in writing this book is to record the first 125 years of the Christian Police Association, of necessity I have also included the other parts of Catherine Gurney's legacy, although not in so much detail. In between, I have sought to introduce other events that were pertinent to the time and to place them in their historical position. I am sure you will understand that when my personal part in this story begins, I have referred to myself in the third person.

I trust that as you read these things, you might give thanks, not only for Catherine Gurney and those who have followed through with her

Catherine Gurney

vision, but also to the one who inspired her and gave her the strength and dynamic to see it through.

Don Axcell
Spring 2016

Chapter 1

*'When constabulary duty's to be done …
a policeman's lot is not a happy one.'*

Immortal words from the great Victorian lyricist WS Gilbert in *The Pirates of Penzance*. Unfortunately, he didn't propose any solution to improving the situation.

The office of constable can be traced back as far the sixteenth century under the reign of Henry VIII. It is believed that the constables developed from the *Tithesmen* who were responsible for ensuring that the tithe (a tax payable to the church) was paid. It was also obligatory in those days for them to attend services at the Church of England.

Constables worked under the direction of a Justice of the Peace serving summonses, executing warrants, taking charge of prisoners and bringing them before the court. They are often depicted carrying a lantern, a rattle (to draw attention) and a staff with which to protect themselves – a far cry from modern police officers and all the equipment they carry.

We are beginning our journey at the start of the eighteenth century in the Bedfordshire town of Woburn, where, on 7 March 1705, a son, Thomas, was born to John and Hannah Gurney. Records show that this was the same John Gurney who was a miller and the lessee of Crawley Mills in Husborne Crawley.

Thomas was not interested in following his father's footsteps and had more scholarly ambitions. As a young man he obtained a book by William Mason on the art of shorthand, quickly mastering the system and using it to faithfully record sermons. This skill was to have a profound influence on the official reporting of legal and government proceedings in the eighteenth and nineteenth centuries.

Following his marriage to Martha Marsom in Luton in 1730, and working for some years as a schoolmaster in both Luton and Newport Pagnell, he moved to London in 1737. Combining his skills, he taught others Mason's art of shorthand and used it himself to record court proceedings at the Old Bailey. This dexterity led to his appointment as official shorthand writer to the court in 1748, and over the next twenty years it is said that he recorded more than 10,000 cases, although it must be presumed that he had some assistance with this task.

One of the effects of this period of the Industrial Revolution was an increase in crime. With thousands of people converging on towns seeking work, the job of crime prevention and detection was much more difficult. In the country villages everyone was known to each other, and if a crime was committed, the old method of 'hue and cry' was still very effective in bringing the guilty to justice. There were no welfare state benefits to fall back on at this time and with no guarantee of work in the towns, poor housing and starvation led many into a life of crime.

In the same year that Thomas Gurney was appointed to his role at the Old Bailey, another person was about to make his mark. Henry Fielding, a man known for his integrity, was made Chief Magistrate for the City of Westminster. Realising that the Parish Constable system needed to evolve, he recruited a small group of people who operated from his office in Bow

Street and yes, they became known as the Bow Street Runners. Although this non-uniformed group was later improved by Henry's brother John, crime and disorder were still increasing, and as a development of the hue and cry system, the Fieldings enlisted the help of the public by publishing descriptions of crimes and criminals in order to solicit information.

As can be observed, with so much crime there was no shortage of work for the courts.

Thomas Gurney had at least three children, one of whom was Joseph, born in 1744. He was obviously well-schooled in his father's shorthand method, for he succeeded him as official reporter at the Old Bailey. Not content with the status quo, Joseph improved on his father's shorthand method and continued to publish various versions of it. Although not easy to master, it was later used by Charles Dickens, who makes mention of it in Chapter 38 of *David Copperfield*.

Around 1783, Joseph Gurney was appointed Parliamentary Shorthand Reporter, combining this with his work at the Old Bailey and as a publisher of court transcripts, speeches and sermons. Joseph fathered three children, giving one son the names of his maternal grandfather, William Brodie.

William Brodie Gurney was born on Christmas Eve 1777 and was brought up in the family home in south-east London. It is recorded that he received adult baptism at Mays Pond Chapel, Southwark, on 1 August 1796. Following in the footsteps of his father and grandfather, he started work as a shorthand writer in 1803, and in the same year married a

WB Gurney

17

Miss Bentham. William reported quite a number of important cases during his lifetime, including the impeachment of Lord Melville in 1806 and the trial of Queen Caroline in 1820. Meanwhile, his elder brother, John, had also been engaged with the law, but in a different way. He became a lawyer, and at the pinnacle of his career served as a baron (judge) in the Court of the Exchequer, a court which eventually became part of the King's Bench Division of the High Court.

The progress of maintaining law and order continued during this period. The roads on the outskirts of London were plagued with highwaymen, and in an effort to eradicate this threat the Chief Magistrate, Sir Richard Ford, reintroduced the Bow Street Horse Patrol which had been formed by Sir John Fielding but later disbanded. As a result, the highwaymen returned. Together with a subsequently added foot patrol, they wore a blue coat with yellow buttons, blue trousers, black boots, a tall black leather hat and white gloves. It could be said that they were the first 'boys in blue', but another distinctive part of their dress, a scarlet waistcoat, earned them the nickname of Robin Redbreasts. These were the first uniformed police in the country and came under the control of the Home Secretary.

William Gurney was passionate about his faith and was heavily involved in Christian work. Five years after his baptism he founded the Mays Pond Sunday School, and two years later was present at the inauguration of the Sunday School Union becoming successively its secretary, treasurer and president. When the Westminster Auxiliary of the British and Foreign Bible Society was formed in 1812, he was elected to the committee and later became secretary. Closely involved in the work of the Baptist denomination, he became treasurer of Stepney College in 1828, and of their Foreign Missions in 1835. He also had more than a passing interest in the anti-slavery movement.

William had several children, but our focus will be on Joseph, who was born on 15 October 1804 in London and named after his grandfather. He continued in the family profession, succeeding his father as official shorthand writer to the Houses of Parliament in 1849. Joseph also had a firm faith and was known as a biblical scholar. For many years he served the committee of the Religious Tract Society, also acting as treasurer to Regent's Park Baptist College, the successor to the college at Stepney. He devoted much time to writing biblical commentaries, which were well received.

While all this activity was taking place in the Gurney household, historical events were pushing forward much-needed changes to policing. In 1815, the Napoleonic War had ended and survivors returned home seeking both accommodation and jobs. Industrialisation had only added to the shortage of employment and the overall situation led to unrest and rioting. The absence of a proper Police Force meant that riots and serious disorder had to be dealt with by the army, who were not known for a soft approach. Perhaps the worst example of military violence against the civil population occurred in 1819. Mounted soldiers turned on a large crowd in Manchester, and it was reported that they killed twelve and injured 400 people. It became known as the Peterloo Massacre.

Into this period of rising crime and civil unrest came a promising young politician, Sir Robert Peel. At the age of twenty-four he was a rising star in the Tory Government and was appointed Chief Secretary for Ireland. In this position he introduced legislation that would lead to the formation of the Royal Irish Constabulary, and he put that experience to good use on returning to England. He accepted the post of Home

Secretary and immediately set about reorganising the criminal code. In 1829, the Metropolitan Police Act was passed, and on 29 September that year, the first 1,000 new police started their street patrols. Due to their association with the Home Secretary they quickly picked up the nicknames of 'Peelers' or 'Bobbies'.

Constables in the new police had to be six feet fall and have no history of any wrongdoing. They worked seven days a week for the sum of £1 and were granted five days' unpaid holiday a year. Their uniform was not dissimilar to the old Bow Street Patrol, but without the red waistcoat. They were dressed to look more like civilians and less like the military, and they were required to wear their uniforms both on and off duty.

Sir Robert Peel was insistent on a civilian Police Force, emphasising that 'The police are the public and the public are the police; the police being only members of the public who are paid to give full time attention to duties which are incumbent on every citizen in the interests of community welfare and existence'.[2] He set out the following nine principles which were to be the foundation of policing:

1. The basic mission for which the police exist is to prevent crime and disorder.

2. The ability of the police to perform their duties is dependent upon public approval of police actions.

3. Police must secure the willing cooperation of the public in voluntary observance of the law to be able to secure and maintain the respect of the public.

4. The degree of cooperation of the public that can be secured diminishes proportionately to the necessity of the use of physical force.

5. Police seek and preserve public favour not by catering to public opinion but by constantly demonstrating absolute impartial service to the law.

6. Police use physical force to the extent necessary to secure observance of the law or to restore order only when the exercise of persuasion, advice and warning is found to be insufficient.

7. Police, at all times, should maintain a relationship with the public that gives reality to the historic tradition that the police are the public and the public are the police; the police being only members of the public who are paid to give full-time attention to duties which are incumbent on every citizen in the interests of community welfare and existence.

8. Police should always direct their action strictly towards their functions and never appear to usurp the powers of the judiciary.

9. The test of police efficiency is the absence of crime and disorder, not the visible evidence of police action in dealing with it.

Around this time, Joseph Gurney married his first wife, Emma Rawlings, with whom he had several children. Sadly, their daughter Mary was only six years old when her mother died, just four years after Queen Victoria had ascended to the throne. But Mary developed a real thirst for knowledge, becoming proficient in at least five languages. Having assisted in the home schooling of her younger siblings, she became involved in voluntary work but still maintained a strong interest in education. This led to her playing a leading part in the founding of the Girls' Public Day School Company (now the Girls' Day School Trust).

Joseph Gurney

Chapter 2

Although London had its new Metropolitan Police, the rest of the country maintained the old system of Justices of the Peace and Parish Constables. Towns were growing very fast and conditions were very poor. The Municipal Corporations Act, passed in 1835, required the boroughs and cities outside London to set up their own Police Forces along the same lines as the metropolis. Progress was very slow, there was little incentive to become a constable, and the conditions of service in these new, rural Forces were just as bad as those in London.

There was great inequality in this society, dominated as it was by the rigid class system of 'upstairs downstairs'. Few cared about the welfare of the man in blue as long as he did his job. If he became ill and was unfit for work, there was no sick pay to fall back on. Times were hard.

Victorian London would see immense changes, but at the start of her reign Queen Victoria presided over a country that, for many of her subjects, was a sea of misery and poverty. In this period of history we find Joseph Gurney. Joseph was widowed in 1842, leaving him with the responsibility of a young family. However, he soon married Harriet Tritton of Norwood with whom he increased the size of his family.

They were living in Lavender Hill, Battersea, when

his daughter Catherine was born on 19 June 1848. Formal education, even for middle-class families, was still the prerogative of the male line, and so Catherine commenced her education at home. It is said that when a governess replaced her older sister Mary as her tutor, she wept bitterly. With the interest and encouragement of her father, education was a significant part of her upbringing.

There were no women's colleges in those days, and the women's suffrage movement was still in its infancy. But Catherine had a strong personality, untiring energy and a thirst for knowledge, all of which assisted her in obtaining a well-rounded upbringing. The family had moved from Lavender Hill to Kingston Road, Wandsworth, to a house called Birdhurst, next door to the Royal Hospital for Incurables (now the Royal Hospital for Neuro-disability). They were still living there when the 1871 census was recorded, but subsequently moved to Tyndale Lodge on Wimbledon Parkside.

As a young woman, Catherine found the same strong faith that had motivated the lives of her father and grandfather. Having accepted that Jesus Christ was her Lord and Saviour, she realised that she needed to put her faith into practice. With a strong sense of duty, she commenced her charitable work among the working-class people of Wandsworth, not far from her home. Conditions in towns were dire for many of these people. Disease was commonplace, much of it due to poor diet and inadequate sanitation. Catherine knew,

Young Catherine

23

however, that changing outward circumstances was not enough; there had to be a change of heart and, to that end, she started a Bible class for men.

Around this time she became interested in police officers. Returning from her efforts in Wandsworth, it was often a dark and lonely walk to her home near Wimbledon Common, and she was grateful for the protection afforded by the officers whom she encountered along the way. She often said that it was the feeling of gratitude that made her long to do something for those who, in their long hours of duty, both night and day, had to endure many dangers and temptations without the appreciation of those they served.

The class system was rigidly entrenched in British society, and even within the Christian community it seemed to be an accepted fact that each was born to their own station in life. This is aptly demonstrated in a verse (now omitted) of the hymn 'All Things Bright and Beautiful', published in 1848:

> *The rich man in his castle*
> *The poor man at his gate*
> *God makes them high and lowly*
> *And ordered their estate.*[3]

The latter half of the nineteenth century saw the beginnings of social change. Consciences were stirred, and during this era many great philanthropic works were to find their origin. Many of the charities started in this period were inspired by Christian leaders, most of whom came from non-conformist backgrounds. In this arena were men such as Lord Shaftesbury who had a great effect on employment law, William Booth who opened 'Food for the Millions' shops (soup kitchens) and founded the Salvation Army, and

Thomas Barnardo of whom it is said that by the time of his death, his homes had sheltered around 60,000 children.

On 12 August 1879, Joseph Gurney died and the family moved from their Wimbledon home to Resington Lodge, 11 Ladbroke Terrace, Kensington, an area better known today as Notting Hill, bringing them nearer the family business in Holborn. It was also in close proximity to the new London Underground railway which would soon complete an inner Circle Line.

Catherine's earlier longing to do something for the police now began to take root. She records that she started 'spiritual work among the police of the Metropolis ... which became known as the International Christian Police Association (ICPA)' in about 1880. The story is told that one Sunday afternoon she offered a small Christian tract to a young policeman near her home. Seeing what it was, he said to her, 'What! Do you think a policeman has a soul?' In her quiet way she replied, 'Why, of course he has!' eliciting the response, 'Well, you are the first person who ever thought so!' Catherine knew that each person was a holistic being (body, mind and spirit) and that to neglect one part jeopardised the whole. Her first instinct was to ensure that the spiritual aspects of life were right, as this would have a profound effect on the lives of individuals.

A woman of seemingly tireless energy, founding the ICPA was just the beginning. Realising she could not do all that was required on her own, she enlisted the help of family and friends. She also received assistance from the police themselves and her work was sanctioned by the Commissioners (Metropolitan and City of London Police).

The first badge of the ICPA showed clasped hands in front of a policeman's helmet. The wrist of one hand featured a policeman's duty band, the other wrist was plain. This symbolised firstly a sympathy from those outside the police  to those within, and secondly that as police officers were required to wear their uniforms whether on or off duty, the duty band signified on duty, and the other, off duty, showing full-time commitment.

The work was formalised in February 1883 as the International Christian Police Association, and September saw the first issue of its magazine *On and Off Duty* (*OOD*), sold for the princely sum of one penny. The objective of that first issue was 'to promote Christian life and work amongst a very important class of men'. The appointment of women police did not come about until the First World War (1914–18).

Work among the police was not confined to the London area. Catherine Gurney's friends and associates had started to travel the country and discovered that a ministry to policemen had already been taking place in Birmingham, Norwich and Windsor for several years. Christian concern for those charged with keeping the peace was spreading rapidly, and the ICPA became the unifying factor for many of those groups.

Many famous spiritual leaders of the time identified

with the work and positively encouraged it. It was reported that on 13 December 1883, forty members of the Leicester Borough Police Force attended a tea at Melbourne Hall provided by the minister, the Rev FB Meyer. A few men who wished to join the ICPA stayed behind to make arrangements for the formation of a branch.

By the time of the first Annual Meeting in March 1884, there were 719 members. Throughout the year the work spread even further, with reports of meetings in Aberdeen, Belfast, Edinburgh, Glasgow and Swansea. Even though these reports convey a picture of much public support for the police, this has to be tempered by the fact that many in the working classes still saw them as oppressors.

Information about the ICPA continued to spread far and wide, and in early 1885 a letter was received from a police officer in Toronto, Canada, indicating that they had received some of the early copies of *OOD* and were hopeful that they might soon start a branch there. Within a short space of time there were reports of ICPA branches in Singapore and Tasmania.

The Annual Meeting in 1885 was quite an event. It was

held for the second year running at the Exeter Hall on the north side of the Strand, central London. This venue, owned by the YMCA, had been the centre for large meetings concerned with the abolition of slavery. It had both a large and small hall, the former able to accommodate over 3,000 people. While the first Annual Meeting filled the small hall, the organisers of the second 'had the joy of seeing

Exeter Hall

27

crowds assemble before the door in the Strand, and of seeing the large hall well filled with a bona fide police congregation, as comparatively few were present except members of the Force and their wives'.

Social concern for the police continued to be a strong platform for Catherine Gurney. In October 1885, an 'Institute for policemen' was opened in central London within a few yards of St James's Park. It was open every day from noon until 10pm as 'a place for rest, recreation, reading, conversation, or refreshment for any member of the Police Force or police recruit'. Bible classes were held twice a week and lectures were delivered at frequent intervals. The very first meeting was presided over by an Assistant Commissioner.

Central to Catherine's Christian life was the practice of prayer. Naturally this manifested itself in her work with and for the police. January 1886 saw the first call for a Day of Prayer for the police. The call went to those inside and outside the police, and was taken up right across the country.

In 1887, Queen Victoria celebrated her Golden Jubilee, and Catherine Gurney wanted to mark this in some special way. She had always been supportive of the Metropolitan and City Police Orphanage but was concerned that there was nothing similar for the provincial Police Forces. A report was commissioned and recommendations made which would set in motion this new venture.

With the welfare of the police at the forefront of her mind, Catherine had arranged for an officer to be admitted to an ordinary convalescent home for a period of two or three weeks. She was most surprised when he returned a few days later. On enquiring why he was not still there, the officer explained that the home was all right, but in the next bed to him was a man he had previously arrested and that he did not find that conducive to sleep! This seed of an experience was to germinate and sprout into the idea of a convalescent home specifically for police officers.

Up until this time, the work had been run from Catherine Gurney's home in Notting Hill, but in that Jubilee year, an office was rented at 18 Adam Street on the south side of the Strand.

The overseas work continued with reports of branches in Tasmania and Singapore, but the main emphasis in *OOD* was on the work in the UK. Articles about travel overseas were included to broaden the minds of officers who were unlikely to be able to go abroad themselves. As there was no plethora of legislation to overwhelm the police, from time to time the magazine contained articles about new Acts of Parliament. Factual reports gave a picture of serious crime, and included the statistics that in the nine years ending 31 December 1886, two policemen were fatally wounded by burglars in the Metropolitan Police District, with a further thirteen woundings nationally. During that period, fourteen burglars were found to be carrying firearms when they were arrested.

Jubilee year would not end well for the police, as there had been massive confrontation with demonstrators from the new socialist movements in Trafalgar Square. Many of those demonstrating were beaten with truncheons and multiple arrests were made. It was reported that two men later died from their injuries. Although ICPA literature did not mention the riots, there was a report that an award of ten guineas was made to 'Inspector Livingston, who sustained very serious injuries during the late riots'.

Elsewhere, the Association was growing in strength and an annual autumn conference was established in the north of the country and in Scotland. Following a gathering held in Glasgow in 1887, a former magistrate, Bailie Dickson, commented on the work of the ICPA that 'whilst the sailors were catered for by the work of Miss Weston, few seemed to have specially thought of our policemen until taken up by Miss Gurney. I trust their cause may prosper'.

Social concern for police officers and their families continued alongside what might be considered more spiritual activity. Steps had been taken to ascertain the needs of the different Police Forces in the north of England to test the feasibility of a northern police orphanage.

In order to maintain a spiritual focus for the work, several offshoots were started. The Police Bible Reading Union was designed to promote the daily study of the Bible by police officers and their families. A Police Temperance Union was started to encourage total abstinence because of the many examples of officers losing their jobs as a result of being drunk. Completing a trio of activities was the Police Missionary Union, aimed at supporting the work of missionaries going overseas, and also missionary work among the Police Forces.

Communication was as vital then as now for getting a quick response, and the ICPA magazine reported in March 1889 on new technology for the police:

> The experiment tried in Islington for communication between civilians and police has proved a great success. The signals are somewhat similar to the fire alarms, and in response to the calls from any post, an already horsed van is promptly driven from Upper Street police station. A prisoner was taken at Highbury Barn, the ambulance telegraphed for, and the man in the dock in 15 minutes, the distance traversed being about a mile and a half. When completed there will be a telephonic communication whereby the Inspectors at the police station will be able to communicate with the police and vice versa. Already

several lives have been saved as a consequence of prompt dealing with would-be suicides.

A new and improved method of communication between police stations is shortly to be introduced in the shape of the now well-known tape telegraph instruments. Among other reforms introduced by the new Commissioner, many of the reports are now typewritten instead of manuscript.

Sadly, early in 1889 Catherine Gurney's mother, Harriet, died. Whilst Catherine could lay claim to be the 'mother' of the ICPA, others accorded this accolade to her mother:

> It has pleased our Heavenly Father to remove from among us, after a few days' illness, one who may truly be called the 'mother' of the Christian Police Association, Mrs Joseph Gurney of Notting Hill. From the time of her coming to Notting Hill in 1880 Mrs Gurney had taken a great interest in the police of the neighbourhood, an interest evinced in many practical ways. In December 1882 as the result of much waiting upon the Lord ICPA was first really proposed and after a preliminary committee in January 1883 the first meeting in connection with the movement was held by Mrs Gurney's kind invitation at her house Resington Lodge in February. The work spread rapidly throughout London and from London to the provinces; still Resington Lodge, which had been its birthplace always continued to be regarded as its centre.

In an account of the funeral at Trinity Presbyterian Church at Notting Hill where she had been a member, it is noted that the coffin was borne by eight members of the ICPA and that afterwards the remains were conveyed to Norwood Cemetery. The burial service at the grave was read

Harriet Gurney

31

by Mrs Gurney's youngest son, the Rev ET Gurney, Rector of Chillenden, and the Rev Dr Angus of Regent's Park College, her brother-in-law, also spoke a few words and offered prayer.

Far from ceasing at Harriet's death, the work among the police seemed to gain new impetus.

That same year, the ICPA office moved a short distance from 18 Adam Street to 1a Adelphi Terrace. This fine old building, formerly home to the Junior Garrick Club, stood on the corner of Adam Street within five minutes' walk of Bow Street Police Office and ten minutes' from the Law Courts. The plan to open a Police Institute at Adelphi Terrace was accomplished in April 1889, just a few weeks after the death of Harriet Gurney.

Adelphi Terrace

With all this activity in London, things had not been static in the rest of the country. The Sheffield Branch of the ICPA had opened a Police Institute in what had formerly been a public house. Needless to say, it had undergone a complete transformation. Meanwhile, Mary Hopkinson in Salford had enlisted the help of friends, and through persistence, an orphanage had been opened for the benefit of the Manchester and Salford Police Forces.

With a new decade came new effort. On Monday 17 March 1890, the new Southern Police Orphanage and Seaside Home was opened at 51 Clarendon Villas, West Brighton, where police officers attending were charged eight shillings per week (about forty pence). The opening ceremony was performed by Countess Lady Chichester, who told how her sympathies for the police had been stirred and deepened by attending a meeting of the Christian Police Association. When the Rev CH Spurgeon addressed the Annual Meeting of the ICPA in Exeter Hall that year, he spoke on the subject 'Why should a policeman be a true Christian?' starting,

Clarendon Villas

'When I was a small boy I always had a great awe of the police, and I feel something of that upon me now.' He added humorously, 'I feel as if I am under police surveillance.'

Before the close of 1890, two more Police Institutes had been opened by ICPA groups, one in Everton Road, Liverpool and the other at 1 Grove Place, Swansea.

Early 1891 saw much activity in Ireland, with a conference in Dublin and another in Belfast held at the Sandes Soldiers Home, and which Catherine Gurney attended with a Miss Thompson and the Misses Garratt of Dublin.

Ever one to keep a challenge before people, Catherine set out four points, suggesting that every ICPA member should be:

1. converted – not merely a Christian in name but truly born again
2. conscientious – not just converted
3. consistent – standing firm as one whole person, not double-minded
4. courageous.

She was also keen that there should be supportive outreach, suggesting that 'it would be very helpful to the life of the different branches if those who are prospering and are near a failing branch, or a new branch, or one still in the future, could … go over two or three at a time and visit by arrangement'.

In July 1891, the Southern Convalescent Home separated from the orphanage as all the space was required for police officers, the orphans going to 11 Goldstone Villas, West Brighton. Later that year, Catherine travelled to the United States of America to attend conventions in Washington and Boston, sending back prayer requests for great blessing on members of the Police Forces of those cities.

While addressing a meeting in Newhaven, Connecticut, where an ICPA branch had been formed, Catherine remarked:

> About 10 years ago I first realised how much policemen were doing for humanity and how little they are appreciated. We expect them to guard our homes and business places, and to protect us in a wonderfully perfect manner. They endure the storms and the keen blasts of winter and are exposed to the heat of summer. Often they endanger their lives and more often they risk their health. If they ever make a mistake, a great deal is said against them; and I came to wonder what I could do for them. I knew something of the Police Force in the District in which I resided. I thought the first thing I could do was to pray, which I did, and soon after talked on the subject with several friends, and they prayed. We began to hold meetings which were attended by policemen and their friends and others who were interested. At the first meeting held there were six persons present. At a meeting held soon afterwards, there were 60 persons present. I am no missionary, only a traveller interested in the welfare of policemen.

Continuing her journey in the north-east of the USA, she crossed into Canada where a new branch was started in Toronto, and on 1 March 1892 they opened a Police Institute at 11 Westgate Street.

Meanwhile, back in the UK, work on the new Police Seaside Home in West Brighton was continuing. On 29 October 1892 the memorial stone was laid, the ceremony being conducted by Her Royal Highness the Princess Christian of Schleswig-Holstein, the fifth child of Queen Victoria. With her great interest in nursing it was not surprising that she had been asked and consented to undertake the task.

Following an address from the Countess of Chichester, Her Royal Highness responded:

> I am deeply sensible of, and grateful for, the kind words which you, Lady Chichester, have just read to me on behalf of the Trustees and Committee of the Police Seaside Home, and I beg you to accept my warmest thanks and the assurance of the great gratification it affords me to be present here today. The work in furtherance of which I have been allowed to take part is one which needs no words to commend it to general support. We owe so much to the police that one rejoices to see some special effort made for their welfare.

Nine months later, on 21 July 1893, the new home in Portland Road was officially opened by the patroness, the Countess of Chichester, although the work was finished and the building occupied well beforehand, with thirty-two visitors enjoying the facilities. Nearly £9,500 had been raised by public subscription to fund the project, but further funding would be required to increase the capacity to fifty-two by furnishing the top floor rooms.

Portland Road

Such was the interest in the home that some 600 Metropolitan Police Officers and wives attended the opening.

At the tenth anniversary of the ICPA in 1893, it could truly be called an international association, as there was now work among the police in America, Canada, Australia, Africa, China, India and Ceylon. A report had also been received of a meeting held at the Calcutta Central Police Station, with more officers signing up as members. In Cape Town the work was carried on in conjunction with the Cape General Mission, with officers appreciating the 'warmth and sympathy that was offered'.

An indication of just how much the work of the Association was appreciated was evident when Miss Elizabeth Grenfell died. She had been at the forefront of Christian work in Swansea, and honorary secretary of the branch there. The announcement of her death caused widespread, heartfelt regret. It was reported that over 12,000 people were present at her funeral.

There had been a growing requirement to cater for police orphans. Since they had moved out of accommodation at Clarendon Villas, numbers had grown and the committee had been unable to find suitable premises in Brighton or elsewhere in Sussex. As an interim measure, a large house and cottage were leased at Sutton Lodge Farm, Brighton Road, Sutton, Surrey.

Less than a year later, in March 1895, they had moved again to a house at Gatton Point, London Road, Redhill, Surrey. The funding for these premises had come from Miss Bell of Park Hill, Tooting, who had been very supportive of the home at West Brighton when the work had commenced. To reflect the wider catchment area now being served, the name was changed from 'Southern' to 'Provincial' Police

Orphanage. At the time of the official opening, nineteen children were accommodated, seven of whom were both fatherless and motherless.

Provincial Police Orphanage

The benefit of convalescent homes specifically for police officers was now widely recognised. In June of the same year, Ladywell Cottage, situated on the shore of St Margaret's Bay between Inverkeithing and North Queensferry in Scotland, was formally opened by the Countess of Moray. The home had been made possible by the generosity of Sheriff and Mrs Gillespie from Glasgow. Mr Boyd, then Chief Constable of Glasgow, thanked the sheriff and hoped it would become a national institution for Scotland. It was noted at the time that the charges would be slightly less than those for the Brighton home as 'money goes further in Fife than it does in Brighton'. Sadly, the home was only open for seven years, as the land had been compulsorily purchased by the Government and the Gillespies had moved from the area.

Chapter 3

A new century is born. A new era begun. But one that was soon to be overshadowed by the death of Queen Victoria on 22 January. *OOD* contained a lengthy memorial to this beloved monarch and a pledge of allegiance to the new king; although it was another eighteen months before his coronation.

Catherine Gurney's first letter of the new century encourages readers to join the Police Scripture Reading Union. Seeking to promote reading of the Bible among those who would not normally open its pages, she says, 'In joining this Union you are not making any profession of religion, which perhaps you would not feel to be real; you are not taking any vow; you are simply saying that you want to know more of God's holy Word, which is your inheritance as much as that of anyone else in the world.'

Bible-reading cards were available from the *OOD* office, and for one shilling (5p), a Bible could be obtained in one of three versions – the Authorised, the Revised or the Roman Catholic Douay version. As Catherine said, 'The question is not which version I read, but do I read it as God's word to me, as "my Father's letter", and am I prepared as I read to abide by it and to follow its teaching?'

Reports from overseas work among the police were

received from time to time. Towards the end of 1901 the following report from the USA reads:

> As a branch of the International Christian Police Association we, the New York Branch, send greetings to the Autumnal Conference of the parent association. The visit to our City in 1891 of Miss Gurney and Mrs Walker was followed by the formation of the police band of prayer taking for their motto 'Call unto me and I will answer thee and show thee great and mighty things which thou knowest not' (Jeremiah 33 v 3). Many members of this band have met for prayer several times every week and from this sprung the New York Christian Police Association under the leadership of Miss S R Kendall. Rooms were taken in December 1892 at 235 West Thirtieth Street and opened as reading and meeting rooms which are still used. Owing to local conditions the work cannot be carried on as it is in Great Britain and her colonies and our progress has been slowed. A meeting is held every Sunday, Tuesday, Friday and Saturday at 235 West Thirtieth Street and every Friday at the YMCA Rooms in Harlem and our attendance has increased largely during the present year.

Further north, the ICPA work in Toronto was flourishing and a flood of reports from there were included in the UK magazine. In addition there were regular accounts of the thriving work in Dublin, Belfast, Glasgow and Edinburgh, complementing work elsewhere.

It was not just in the English-speaking world that the ICPA was to be found. The *Japan Times* carried a report of ICPA meetings in November 1902 at the YMCA building in Kanda. The

ICPA Group, Kanda, Japan

headquarters was in Kumamoto and there were between 700 and 800 members across the country. The chief officials of both the Ken Province and city had commended the work of the Association.

With Police Institutes well established in major cities across the UK, such was their popularity that some needed larger premises. This was the case for Leeds, where a small institute had been run in Hanover Street since 1897 to much acclaim. On 10 February 1903, a new Leeds Police Institute was opened by the Lady Mayoress (Mrs Ward) at Oxford Chambers, Victoria Square.

Northern Police Convalescent Home

That same year saw the official opening of the Northern Police Convalescent Home at Harrogate on 11 May, conducted by the Viscount and Viscountess Mountgarret. Police officers in the north of England had been taking a great interest in this project and had raised two-thirds of the purchase price themselves. As with the Southern Convalescent Home, this was going to be a facility that would be well used and of great benefit to the Police Service.

Appeals for funding for designated items were made on a regular basis through the magazine. Sometimes it was a new piece of furniture for one of the orphanages or perhaps a bed for one of the convalescent homes. At other times, appeals in support of a specific building project were made through the pages of the magazine. In November 1903, to celebrate the twenty-first year of the Association, a Million Shilling Fund was launched for the purpose of providing a permanent and suitable Police Institute for the metropolis and also to assist the work of the orphanages and convalescent homes. At that time, the headquarters of the ICPA was still sharing premises with the Police Institute in leased accommodation at Adelphi Terrace, central London. Of the £50,000 this fund hoped to raise, by March 1906 it had only reached £500. With the comment 'every little helps', it still seemed that there was a reluctance to put the various works that Catherine Gurney had started on a sound financial footing.

Reports from work overseas continued to come in. Miss Riddell in Japan commented that

> the Japanese are never able to understand how it is that though their population is about the same as ours, they have only 21,000 paupers while we have about 1 million. The difference is due to the Japanese attitude towards old age and parenthood. Most of their few paupers are children or elderly people whom earthquakes have deprived of their breadwinners. Old age is all but sacred in Japan.

The twelfth Annual Report from the ICPA in Toronto mentioned their regular meetings every Wednesday afternoon, which had an average attendance of twenty-one members. They gave thanks to God that by his 'good guiding and the courtesy of Chief Grasett and the Board of Police Commissioners, the gymnasium days have this year been changed, leaving Wednesday free for all those not on active duty to attend the Bible class if they choose, and we are indeed glad that many are availing themselves of this opportunity'.

Educational help for police examinations often featured in the magazine. In one issue there were punctuation hints for composition, which we might well take note of today.

> The Comma. This *stop* is often said to be the most important used in punctuation, for if it is inserted in the wrong place, it may render obscure or even change entirely the meaning of a sentence. The following is a familiar example of how the changing of the position of a comma may alter the meaning implied in a sentence:
>
> A. The sergeant says, the constable is a fool.
> B. The sergeant, says the constable, is a fool.
>
> In A the sergeant makes the statement; but, by altering the position of the comma, as in B, the constable has turned the tables on the sergeant and makes the statement.

One of the most notable events of the first decade of the twentieth century was the revival in Wales. It had certainly caught the attention of Catherine Gurney, who referred to it on more than one occasion in her monthly letter. In March 1905 she said:

> We have all heard and read a good deal of the revival in Wales. Men of all creeds and parties are looking at it with interest, for they cannot help being interested in its results, even if they feel little sympathy with the revival itself. Quite recently the Chief Constable of Flintshire, in reporting a decided decrease of drunkenness, attributed it to the effect of the revival, and the same might be said of other counties. If a revival is to have permanent results, there must be four prominent marks of its power on men. First, conviction of sin. Second, an appreciation and acceptance of the work of Christ for us. Third, an appreciation of the presence of God, and consequently a

desire to pray. Fourth, there will be a manifestation of the fruit of the spirit. What is our responsibility with regard to it? Is God only the God of Wales? Is his power limited to certain places or people? Nay, God so loved the world – you and me, and everybody. If with all your hearts ye truly seek Him, ye shall surely find Him.

Many stories of changed lives emerged from the revival, and Catherine recounted the following:

How a more delicate sense of justice sprang up in many hearts amidst the nearer more frequent daily approaches of the community to God may be seen in such incidents as follow. At Pontypridd, a brewer clerk handed in his resignation, giving as his reason that he had been converted. In the Rhondda Valley, several publicans being converted cleared out of the business as soon as possible. One man who kept a large hotel, a most profitable concern in mid Rhondda has, since his conversion and renunciation of the trade, written a most beautiful Welsh hymn.

I heard a jeweller confess that he used to sell white sapphires as diamonds and paste as pearls, and that he used to charge three shillings and sixpence for repairing a watch when the hairspring was simply twisted but, he added, all that is changed since the revival. In one instance a cook who was brought to Christ at one of the meetings, went to her mistress a few days after and told her she knew she had not served her faithfully in the past and she asked her mistress to allow her to give one year's service without wages as compensation! The mistress says she has never seen such work done in her house as now. (May 1906)

It was still a feature of the annual ICPA meetings in London, to have a notable Christian speaker. In 1905, the singing at the meeting was led by a renowned American singer and writer, Mr CM Alexander, and the message given by Dr RA Torrey, the noted American evangelist, who had previously been associated with DL Moody and had been his successor at his church in Chicago. On addressing the meeting, Dr Torrey spoke on the subject 'What does it cost not to be a Christian?' and he took as his points:

1. Not to be a Christian costs the sacrifice of peace of conscience and peace of heart.
2. Not to be a Christian costs the sacrifice of joy.
3. Not to be a Christian costs the sacrifice of hope.
4. Not to be a Christian costs the sacrifice of the highest manhood or of the highest womanhood.
5. Not to be a Christian costs the sacrifice of God's favour.
6. Not to be a Christian costs the sacrifice of Christ's acknowledgement in the world to come.
7. Not to be a Christian costs the sacrifice of eternal life.

In defining a Christian he said, 'By a Christian I understand any man, woman or child who accepts Jesus Christ as his or her personal saviour, who surrenders to him as his or her Lord and Master, confesses him as such publicly before the world, and strives to live to please him in everything day by day.'

The advancement of the ICPA overseas continued, often due to those who had previously heard of the work in the UK, and then travelled abroad whether for work or Christian service. After eleven years of praying for an opportunity, a branch was started in 1905 in Kingston, Jamaica, followed shortly afterwards by another in Chapelton. Around the same time, the following letter had been received from a Douglas Wood in Johannesburg.

> I think this is the first time I have ever written to On and Off Duty though it is a paper I have seen and read

many a time. But now I want to ask the prayers of your readers for our brothers in the Force out here in South Africa, and especially in this city of Johannesburg. Even here where Satan's seat is fixed so strongly, God has his witnesses among the police and your paper is taken and read by quite a number. A meeting is held for them the first Friday of every month in the hall of the South Africa General Mission, which I have the honour of taking and we want to ask for your prayers that this meeting may grow, and that others may spring out of it perhaps in the different barracks where it is easier to reach our brothers. We are looking forward to a visit from Mr and Mrs Small and would ask the prayers of friends at home that God will greatly bless their visit to this city and enable us, through their presence amongst us, to get into touch with many more of our brothers in the Force.

While many readers will be able to identify with some part of this book, it was of particular interest to the author when researching, to find in the ICPA magazine among the various reports of In Memoriams, etc, a happy event which must have been quite a rarity in those days – a Golden Wedding. It was reported that

on September 23rd last, Mr and Mrs David Carter of 28 Holdernesse Road, Upper Tooting, celebrated their Golden Wedding having been joined in wedlock in 1855 by the late Canon Nicholl at Streatham. They have had six sons and three daughters but only two survive. Mr Carter served 26 years in the Metropolitan Police and for 18 of those he was stationed in the neighbourhood of Elephant and Castle. It is recorded that he was converted whilst in the Force and was one of the first to join the Christian Police Association.

(NB The author delivered newspapers in Holdernesse Road as a young teenager but the house referred to no longer exists.)

There was sorrow in the Gurney household with the sudden and unexpected death of Catherine's brother, Joseph John Gurney, JP, in Newcastle upon Tyne on 3 December 1906. Joseph had been a trustee of the ICPA as well as having an active interest in the Baptist Missionary Society. He was sorely missed by Catherine, as he had been her constant advisor.

In an article entitled 'Taking Steps' in March 1907, there would appear to be the first statement of evangelical faith accepted by the Association. In a lecture by Dr Pierson at the Exeter Hall he is quoted as saying that he devoutly wished that before the place was demolished or perverted to secular uses,

> there might be called to meet there one great acumenical [*sic*] council when from all quarters of the world there might come together evangelical believers in a solemn and unanimous confession of their unalterable faith in the full inspiration of the Word of God, in the deity and infallibility of our Lord Jesus Christ as a Teacher, in the reality of his virgin birth, miraculous resurrection, and all sufficient atoning death.

He wished to see that

> tens of hundreds of thousands of believers still hold to the divine inspiration of the Word of God, to the miraculous birth and resurrection of the Lord Jesus Christ, to the all sufficiency of his atoning blood, to his name as the only 'name given under heaven among men whereby we must be saved'. These imperilled truths of our day are the only truths that have ever consoled men in the sufferings of their life, guided them in their innumerable perplexities, comforted them in their dying hours, and prepared them for the mysteries of the life to come.

Catherine Gurney's own globetrotting had continued, and in her report at the twenty-fourth Annual Meeting of the ICPA she talked of work among the police in Paris and of the interest stirred in her heart by meeting with many *carabineers* and police in Italy. She also reported concerning the Berlin ICPA,

> General-Lieutenant Von Schultz-Endorff, the President of the German Christian Police Association (Bund Christlicher Polizei Beamter) is now 72 years of age but gives all his time and heart to the work. He holds a Bible class in his house and visits other classes in different parts of the city. He has written a very inspiring little book which he has given to more than 100 Generals of his acquaintance to explain to them the work that is being done for policemen.

She was glad to hear that the Bible classes were prospering in Berlin under the guidance of Frauline Von Redern, and that a very successful Annual Meeting had been held.

Campaigning against the evil of alcohol abuse had been firmly linked to the ICPA through the Police Temperance Union, but a campaign against smoking did not emerge until the late twentieth century. However, the magazine of July 1907 contained a report that

> less than three years ago a Chancellor of the Exchequer told the House of Commons that he had ascertained that over 100 million cigarettes are sold weekly in the United Kingdom in penny packets alone! The majority of the buyers are boys and youths, who in the effort to appear manly, are probably ignorant of the fact that Sir Morell Mackenzie, the great throat specialist, declared that of all forms of smoking, cigarette smoking was the most injurious.

From 1908 another change started within the Association. Local branches had been set up and run by Christians in the community, but from this point police officers began taking on the role of branch secretary. It would be some considerable time before this would become the general pattern of local leadership.

The benefits of taking the sea air were widely espoused from the late Victorian period onwards, which was why the first convalescent home and orphanage had been started close to the coast. With the move of the orphanage

SEASIDE HOME, HAYLING ISLAND, HANTS.

Orphans Seaside Home

inland, the Southern Police Orphanage and Seaside Home was opened at Hayling Island in Hampshire to provide the children with seaside outings and holidays. Sales of work were held to support this part of the work.

The ICPA urged the Christian community to support the police and was encouraged when, in 1909, the Bishop of London suggested that an occasional intercession should be made in the churches that the police 'may be helped daily in their difficult work'. This was a theme regularly taken up by Catherine Gurney herself as, whenever she was asked to sign a book, she would always, underneath her name, add 'Pray for the Police'.

The occasional report on innovations that would assist the police and public alike continued in 1910 with an account of 'first aid in the city':

> In London the electric ambulance, used for the speedy conveyance of the injured to hospital, is to the accident precisely what the fire engine is to the fire. As to the vehicle itself, the body was made to the design of the

St John Ambulance Association. It is strongly built of ash, with mahogany panelling, being finished in white enamel, which is relieved by the City Arms and the Geneva Cross. The interior of the ambulance is fitted with two portable stretchers on the left hand side, one above the other. On the opposite side there is a locker running the full length of the vehicle. As many as three or four persons can be accommodated on the lid of this locker in a sitting position, of course, leaving the stretchers free for the badly injured patients.

Within the last two years, there have been erected in the City of London, 52 telephone call boxes for the purpose of summoning the ambulance. These are enamelled white and bear the Geneva Cross in red at the top. They are, for the most part, fixed at places where a constable is on point duty, so that there may be as little delay as possible. The boxes can only be opened by a special key, one of which is carried by every constable. Inside the box there is a call instrument communicating direct with the Head Office of the City Police in Old Jury.

With a report on the death of King Edward VII, it was noted that he was the first monarch to officially recognise the services of the police with the institution of the King's Police Medal to be given as a reward for conspicuous bravery and long and faithful service. The silver medal had, on one side, an effigy of the King and on the other, a representation of a city with an armed figure at its gate holding a huge sword and shield. Beneath were the words 'To guard my people'. That year it had been presented to thirty-six police officers.

In that same year Florence Nightingale had died, leaving a legacy that would have a profound effect on the nursing profession. An anagram of her name, 'Flit on cheering angel', was a most appropriate description of her ministry. It would be almost 100 years later that one of Her Majesty's Inspectors of Constabulary would say, 'the nurses have their Florence

Nightingale and the police have Catherine Gurney and they must never forget her'.

At the end of the year, another significant policing moment took place with the Police (Weekly Rest Day) Act 1910 coming into being to give members of the constabulary one day's rest off duty in every seven. With many officers literally worked to death, it was to be hoped that this might help alleviate the situation.

Less than two years after the shooting of PC William Tyler at Tottenham, the police and public were once again numbed by the outrage in the City of London when five police officers were shot by armed burglars in a single incident. Sadly, three of them, Sergeants Bentley and Tucker and Constable Choate succumbed to their wounds. Demonstrating their support for the men who had shown such self-sacrifice in their duty, crowds packed the streets for the funerals. Such was the intense feeling that there was total silence and men removed hats and caps in respect. It was revealed that the King had sent a personal message of sympathy.

The end of 1910 and the beginning of 1911 saw officers from many Forces being drafted in to police the coal strike in South Wales. It was an arduous and thankless task. The officers were on duty for practically twenty-four hours at a time, and in their off-duty periods were confined in very poor housing. In spite of this, the men apparently complained very little.

No sooner had that strike ended than the City of London had its own problems with the print strike. Overtime was, once again, the order of the day. Single officers were confined to their quarters in case of emergencies, but at least it is recorded that they had comfortable reading and billiard rooms. In view of the severe weather conditions, one chief inspector allowed his men the extra indulgence of going into the police station for hot coffee!

The Annual Meeting of the ICPA in 1911 saw the introduction of another new ministry embraced by the Association – the Pocket Testament League. The League already had over 100,000 members who pledged to carry a Pocket Testament wherever they went and read one chapter a day. A large number of officers at the conference joined the League, and subsequently Pocket Testaments could be obtained from the Association's offices.

King George V had been made aware of the various ministries founded by Catherine Gurney, and in 1911 he graciously consented to be patron of both the Provincial Police Orphanage at Redhill and the Northern Police Orphanage at Harrogate, sending his very best wishes for the success that the Institutions so thoroughly deserved.

There were many committed Christian men and women outside the police, who tirelessly supported the work of the Association. One such was Miss Emma Thompson of Dublin in recalling whose work, Lady Barter of Cork said,

> I thank God for the inspiration of dear Miss Thompson's example. It may be said of her that as she had opportunity she tried to do good to all men, soldiers, prison warders, and others and especially to members of the Royal Irish Constabulary. Her work was so much a personal and individual one that it will be hard for anyone to fill her place; so much of it was done by correspondence, which is indeed almost the only way of reaching the men in many country places. For many years she has carried on the work of the Scripture Union and also undertook to be secretary of the scattered branch of the ICPA.

The work overseas was still advancing with reports from Toronto, New York and Jamaica. The Police Missionary Union supported the work of James Cuthbertson in Japan, and there were regular reports of his progress, particularly among police officers. The Cuthbertson family home was used as a police institute, but sadly in 1913 the house was burnt down. Thankfully everyone was safe.

Branches of the Christian Police Association were set up on a 'town' basis, reflecting the structure of Police Forces across the country at this time. So it was hardly surprising that the Manchester and Salford Branch reported in its autumn conference that they were delighted to welcome representatives from about forty branches. They felt that the conference had left them with a great desire to do more than they had ever done in the service of the Master and to be a vital influence, a real power for good, in the Police Forces. Their report concludes with the words, 'The Association is international, and it is interdenominational, which sounds as if it were indeed very wide embracing and so it is. Yet it is very definite, some might think exclusive, in its conditions of membership, for it requires nothing less than a distinct avowal of Christian discipleship.'

Change can often be slow in coming and those affected may resist it. In 1913, London was given an account of the system of women police in Germany, which had been introduced ten years earlier. While thirty-one towns in Germany employed women police, their duties varied from place to place. Some were performing full police duties, whereas others were involved only in preventative and rescue work with women and children. Although the idea of women police in England was favoured, it took international events to hasten their employment.

Always on the lookout for new innovations that would assist the police to carry out their duties more safely and effectively, the police in Paris had come up with a novel invention. The Prefect of Police issued a circular saying, 'With a view to facilitating the arrest of dangerous criminals and protecting those entrusted with such duties, the Prefecture will always be ready, when necessary to supply special pistols charged with suffocating gases.' It was said that though they were powerful and rapid in action, the pistol left no after-effects. Just to make sure of this, it was reported that Monsieur Gridard, head of the Detective Department, had first tried the gases on himself before allowing his men to use them.

Royal interest in the work of the Association continued when in 1913 Prince and Princess Alexander of Teck paid an official visit to the orphanage at Redhill. In a formal response, the Prince said that their visit was not only to encourage the work, but also to show the interest they took in the Police Forces of Great Britain 'which were second to none'.

Bound up in the history of the Police Institutes, the convalescent homes and the orphanages is the name of Miss Bell of Tooting. Not one to push herself forward, Catherine Gurney was keen to give Miss Bell the credit for the part she had played. In her monthly letter of February 1914 she gave the following tribute:

> Long ago, after God had laid on my heart the great need of an institute for the young men of our Force, the right house (1a Adelphi Terrace), was found and claimed in prayer, but the first step in obtaining it could not be taken without a sum in hand of £200 required within two days. Prayer was made that God would show His will concerning this house by sending or withholding the £200. His answer was plain when Miss Bell, unasked, wrote enclosing a cheque for the sum needed, saying that she knew not why, but she felt constrained to send this by a certain post which brought it to our hands exactly on the day and at the hour it was required. A year later when Miss Griffin

and I were seeking a house at Hove to establish a Police Convalescent Home or an Orphanage, our attention was directed to 51 Clarendon Villas. Our friend Miss Bell, who happened to be in Brighton that day, looked over it with us and then said, 'If you'd like to take this house, I will give you the rent for three years, and will pay for the alterations needed.' So the first Police Convalescent Home and the Southern Police Orphanage were started at once and by the grace of God have continued and prospered. When shortly afterwards the children needed a home of their own, it was the same kind friend who furnished the means to purchase first one little house and then another in Hove and when it was found necessary to remove the Orphanage, it was she who bought the first house for it at Redhill. Nor was the Convalescent Home forgotten, for seeing the need for a much larger house, Miss Bell purchased the site on which it now stands, placing it in the hands of Trustees and liberally helped the building of the new Home, which was opened in 1893. Her great desire in all her giving was that it should be used to the glory of God, and for the welfare both temporal and spiritual of those she desired to serve.

She could not have foreseen the catastrophic events that would soon develop in the country and plunge everyone into the largest war the world had ever known.

Chapter 4

The posturing among European powers was brought to a head when Arch Duke Ferdinand, the heir to the Austro-Hungarian throne, was assassinated whilst on a visit to Serbia on 28 June 1914. This catalyst led to a number of alliances which soon saw all of Europe at war. Because of the global nature of European empires, the war was shortly to envelop the world. Britain's longstanding treaty with Belgium meant that they had an obligation to defend them. When Germany invaded neutral Belgium at the beginning of August that year, Britain was compelled to act and declared war. As a result of this, 'The Great War', 15 million people were killed over the following four years. On 20 August, Bishop J Taylor Smith, the chaplain general, wrote to Catherine Gurney from the war office in the following terms:

> Dear Miss Gurney
> May I, through the columns of your magazine, invite all policemen and others to offer up a prayer at 12 o'clock each day (or night) for those now engaged in fighting for their country? I am sure the knowledge that they are thus being remembered at a given time will be a great source of comfort, hope, and strength to our soldiers and sailors.
> Yours very sincerely,
> J Taylor Smith

One result of the conflict was that many police officers, who were reservists, were mobilised, leaving large gaps in local Forces. To fill these gaps, police pensioners were called up to return to their former occupation. The ICPA magazine expressed the hope that employers would keep the jobs open for the constables when their service in the Forces was no longer required. In her monthly letter for September, Catherine Gurney said,

> I should like to say how much we are thinking of our police reservists, both in the Army and Navy, and of their wives and children. Daily they are remembered in prayer. We would have liked to shake hands with all our reservists as they went, wishing them victory and a safe return. Remember that if you need a convalescent home at any time you will be gladly welcomed at Hove or Harrogate. We have notified the War Office to this effect.

Because of the threat posed by extremists within the UK during this time of war, a number of Forces armed their officers on a regular basis. This did not, however, lead to a general arming of the police. The hostilities inevitably led to casualties and the need for repatriation, treatment and convalescence. In response to this, Catherine Gurney was able to give assurance that at the Police Seaside Home at Hove they had set aside twenty-five beds, and at the Harrogate Police Convalescent Home fifteen beds, all free of charge for the use of police reservists, soldiers or sailors who may be sent home sick or wounded from the war.

By the end of 1914 the war, which many had thought would be short and sharp, was in full flow. News started to arrive from the front and extracts of letters were published in the magazine. Another news item that was to become a regular feature was the 'Roll of Honour', listing the names of police officers who had been called up or enlisted and had subsequently lost their lives. Similarly, a 'For King and Country' page recorded acts of bravery and heroism by those known to the Association, who had gone to war.

The New Year came with countries still locked in hostilities. At home, a special meeting for prayer was held at the Central Police Institute in London on 20 January, at which a short address was given by the Rev Oswald Chambers, then principal of the Bible Training College at Clapham.

Overseas, Sergeant Lilley, formerly of the Cumberland Constabulary and then serving with the Second South Staffordshire Regiment in France, was asked how Christians at home could best help the soldiers. He responded:

> I would urge all Christians to keep on praying earnestly for the men at home and abroad. God has already answered prayer in a wonderful manner, and I believe we shall see yet greater things. I would also urge Christian people to supply every soldier with a Pocket Testament. When the men get to the front they appreciate a Testament ten times more than they did at home.

It is said that the Word of God is powerful to save, and a very practical example of this was an account of how a Pocket Testament in a soldier's pocket had stopped the progress of a bullet which otherwise might have had fatal consequences. There were many similar instances recorded when soldiers were grateful to be carrying God's Word.

The rigours of war did not

Active Service Testament

57

stop the work of the police charities at home and this was duly reported.

> By means of a fund raised among police officials by Dr Halliday, the physician to the Force, the Glasgow police have presented to the Northern Police Convalescent Home at Harrogate a splendid, full sized gramophone with a beautiful cabinet of six dozen assorted records. For the past few years the Glasgow police have had an endowed bed at this home, where members of the Force suffering from rheumatism and other ailments may be received without cost. The gift is very much appreciated.

Meanwhile in the south, at the annual meeting of the Hove Convalescent Seaside Home, it was recorded that the house was more than full having seventy-two patients, including several police reservists and six other soldiers in various stages of convalescence. The meeting was opened with the hymn 'Oh God, Our Help in Ages Past' and with prayer, and was closed with the National Anthem.

Royal interest in the work of Catherine Gurney was not confined to the south of England. In October 1915, there was a private visit to the Northern Police Convalescent Home at Harrogate by Her Royal Highness Princess Victoria (daughter of Princess Christian and granddaughter of Queen Victoria), and Her Imperial Highness, the Grand Duchess George of Russia. They were not concerned with just meeting the staff but chatted to patients in the Day Room, taking an individual interest in everyone who was spoken to.

As the war in Europe continued it was inevitable that ICPA branches would be affected. A report from the Belfast Branch noted that

> Upon restarting our weekly meetings in the Soldiers' Home early in October, we did so with a feeling of sorrow

and loss. We had just received the news that one who had been a loyal member of our ICPA and a regular attender at our meetings and who had been one of our brave men to volunteer last year in the Irish Guards, had succumbed to wounds received in France, and had been called up to higher service. Sergeant Boyd (formerly Constable Boyd of Craven Street) was one whose character demanded respect from all who knew him, and the affectionate regard of those who were his close comrades. Though retiring and unassuming, his manner of life and conversation bore clear and unmistakable testimony to the sincerity of his Christian profession.

They also report that a number of other Belfast Royal Irish Constabulary men had fallen in battle.

With the main focus of attention being near to home, it would have been easy to overlook what was happening elsewhere in the world, but work was continuing among police officers in a variety of places.

The Rev AR Saunders sent a report of his work in China where he was supported by the Royal Irish Constabulary Missionary Union:

Six large cities have been visited by Chinese evangelists several times. Arrangements are now almost completed for the establishment of permanent work in the large and important cities of Soochow and Yangchow. We are able to see results in the definite conversion of men. One sergeant and a constable in Kaoyn have openly declared themselves Christians and have applied for baptism. The son of a sub-inspector and a constable in Taichow Ku have been baptised and three others have applied to the Presbyterian Church there for baptism.

Meanwhile, the ICPA branch in Tokyo reported that a number of officers and a few civilians had been converted to Christianity. Through the valiant work of the police missionary there, several other people had also come under the conviction of their sinful state before God.

God had been using a number of Christian women to minister to the needs of police officers, and it was always a sad occasion when one of them passed away. On 17 May 1917, the Greenock Police Force and members of the community learned of the death of Miss Anna Ritchie, who had served the local branch as treasurer since its inception, subsequently adding to that the role of secretary. Her services to the police were many and extended over thirty years, so it was perhaps no surprise that the Chief Constable and a large contingent of officers attended her funeral in uniform, at the Wesleyan Methodist Church.

Before the year was ended, another milestone marked Catherine Gurney's work. From 1 October she would be known as foundress and president, and on this same date the Rev George Twentyman MA would become general secretary. In her monthly letter for September that year, Catherine wrote,

> After nearly 39 years of work (which began at Wandsworth in 1878), I am thankful to hand over the general work to younger and far more capable hands and am hoping to have more time for individual correspondence and for visiting, as well as for the care of the homes and orphanages, of which I am retaining the honorary secretaryship. Meanwhile I want to bespeak a hearty welcome for our new Secretary in all our branches and throughout the Forces. As a native of Liverpool, of a Cumberland family, and for 16 years a hard-working and much beloved clergyman in the East End of London, he is connected both with the North and South; both with the Metropolis and the Provinces.

The following month the Rev Twentyman wrote his first letter in *OOD* in which he said,

I want you to feel that you are taking into your Association a man in whom you can confide, and one that you can trust with your sorrows and your joys – in fact, a big brother with a big heart and a broad back, or if you like, a padre of your own who will be ready just to do anything that he can to help you in any way!

Rev George Twentyman

Encouraging Christians outside the police to take an interest in their welfare had always been part of the work of the ICPA. It had been known as The Willing Hearted Helpers Band. With the Rev and Mrs Twentyman now installed in the work, this was renamed the Christian Police Association Helpers Guild and Mrs Ethel Twentyman became the chief honorary secretary. Writing about the work, she said, 'Everyone who values the protection and work of our policemen should join our Guild.' An advertisement for the Guild in *OOD* described it as 'A band of friends connected or unconnected with the Police Forces, who recognising the big debt of gratitude the public owe to the men in blue, are willing to pray for them in their difficult work and to wish for any opportunity of a kindly word of action to the police and their families'.

Less than twelve months later, with the war still raging, George Twentyman wanted to do his part, and as missioner and helper with the YMCA, he went off to visit the troops in Salonica. In his absence, his wife acted as deputy secretary.

The provision of care for the welfare of police orphans was not the sole domain of Catherine Gurney. For a number of years there had also been a Metropolitan and City Police Orphanage and this too needed to raise funds for its operation. One such venture was a pamphlet written by Mr Hall Caine called *Policemanship*. Extracts from this were published in the August 1918 issue of the ICPA magazine. The following quotations, painting a glowing picture, were timely considering the events that took place later that month.

> The policeman is the soldier of the street. His enemies are vice and crime. Against these foes he wages a lifelong warfare. He has many victories and some of the greatest of them the world never hears anything about. Perhaps it is taken for granted that a policeman shall do his duty, and die for it if need be. The policeman is the nurse of national morality. His duty is to defend society against the people who decline to be bound by the accepted standard of good conduct. Let us say to the soldier of the street, who spends his life to serve and save us, that in the great spiritual change which the war has brought, making us one nation, one people, one family, we shall henceforth consider it is the sacred duty of the state, and of each and all of us, to look to the welfare of the dear ones he leaves behind.

Wonderful words, but the State had been taking the police for granted. As many officers were serving overseas with the Armed Forces, the pressures on those who remained at home had increased. The cost of living had more than doubled during the war, but a police officer's pay was still only the equivalent of an agricultural worker's. Their leave entitlement had been reduced and some were working nearly 100 hours a week.

Unrest had been growing until on 30 August the unthinkable happened – police officers went on strike – for the first time. The centre of London saw a march of around 12,000 men descend on the seat of government. The Prime Minister, David Lloyd George, had been in France and at once returned home to offer terms that would immediately end the strike.

Less than three months later, on 11 November 1918, the Armistice was signed and the war ended. There was great rejoicing, but much sadness at the monumental loss of life, as Catherine Gurney commented at the time, 'In our thanksgiving, let us remember the hosts of our brothers who have sacrificed their lives in the cause of freedom and righteousness, and the other hosts who will go through the remainder of their days maimed, blinded or enfeebled because (as they would tell you) they only did their duty.'

The war had hastened the introduction of another great change in policing – the employment of women police. A number of Police Forces had already taken on women to perform certain duties, but this was formalised by the Home Office in 1919. In an interview, Miss Damer Dawson, then titled 'Chief of the Women Police', stated that there were chief constables who declared that they could not see what there would be for women police to do after the war. She said, 'We mean to do precisely what policemen have done for women and children in the pre-war days, only we hope to do it a great deal better.' Her confidence was not misplaced, but it was many years before women police had the opportunity to gain chief officer status.

Catherine Gurney had never sought recognition for herself, only for the work with which she was so passionately involved. From those brief encounters with policemen when she lived in Wandsworth, to the starting of the ICPA from her home in Notting Hill, the work had grown rapidly, expanding across the UK and beyond. She had worked tirelessly to provide for the spiritual and temporal welfare of police officers. But recognition did come when, in January 1919, she was made an officer of the Order of the British

Empire (OBE). This brought great joy and satisfaction to all who knew her.

It was now nearly forty years since the work of reaching out to police officers commenced in the home of Harriet Gurney. They say that large oaks from little acorns grow, and this was certainly true for the International Christian Police Association. It has been calculated that Catherine travelled one and a quarter times round the world, not content just to found spiritual work among the police, but also turning her mind to the practical side of a police officer's life. The convalescent homes provided new life for the body and help for the soul, as attested by those who used these facilities. The news of a policeman being shot while on duty, leaving a widow and seven children totally unprovided for, was a catalyst which led to the establishment of the orphanages. All these works were probably unknown to the wider world, but deeply appreciated by those who benefited from them.

The Garratt sisters in South Africa, who had previously been working in Ireland, were still burdened by the request of Catherine Gurney to think of the needs of the police. By June 1919 they expressed the desire that through the spreading work of the ICPA, never again would police officers be able to say that nobody cared for them. It was also their aim to show the practical side of Christianity by starting a small convalescent home by the sea on the Cape Peninsula. They had no funds for this venture, but were prepared to trust God to supply their needs. Their efforts were rewarded

Police Cottage Convalescent Home, SIMONSTOWN, SOUTH AFRICA.

The Aloes

when, by the end of the year The Aloes, meaning 'endurance', was opened at Simonstown.

The autumn of 1919 was eventful in a number of ways. Following the police strike in 1918, the Government had set up a committee under Lord Desborough to look at pay and conditions. One of the recommendations was that there should be a Police Federation to represent officers up to and including the rank of chief inspector. The Government accepted the Desborough Report, a Police Act was passed and the Police Federation established.

Not all were happy with this situation, as the right to belong to a trade union had been removed. A second strike was called, but it did not have widespread support. Strong local support on Merseyside led to rioting which had to be quelled by the military. Two thousand police officers who had gone on strike were all sacked. On the positive side there were pay increases, free housing and a generous pension, subject only to good conduct. The eight-hour working day was established, with additional pay or time off for overtime worked.

During this period there had been considerable unrest in Ireland, where there had been a unilateral declaration of independence. The Irish Republican Army (IRA), led by Michael Collins, began a programme of attacks on UK Government forces. The cities were under control, but in the country areas members of the Royal Irish Constabulary (RIC) took the full force of these attacks. In many isolated rural areas the

Exiles

RIC were forced to abandon their barracks. Shocking figures released in late 1920 showed that up to that time, 117 RIC officers had been killed and 185 wounded. During the same year, over 600 men had resigned from the Force, leaving many areas unprotected and local people open to intimidation, assault and murder, not to mention widespread destruction of property.

Before long the Irish Free State was proclaimed, with six counties in the north becoming Northern Ireland and remaining in the UK. Within two years, the RIC would be disbanded and replaced by the *Garda Siochána* in the south and the Royal Ulster Constabulary in the north.

Alongside serious reporting, helpful advice, spiritual entreaties etc, there was often room for the inclusion of the humorous in the guise of the serious. One such item appeared in the April 1920 edition of *OOD* and was a quotation from a weekly newspaper called *Weekly Dispatch*. The article entitled 'How to Act in Emergencies' carried the following advice:

> The *Weekly Dispatch* symposium, in which various celebrities discussed the way to act in the event of a burglar being found in the house, shows the need for a little advice in case of emergencies. We've penned the following very helpful hints:
>
> The old plan of offering a burglar a cigarette and asking him to take a chair while you telephone to the police is not now so successful as in the past. The best plan is to tackle the fellow right away. For this purpose you should step behind him, take hold of his coat and force it over his face. Then tie his left arm to his right leg across the back. Properly carried out, this method rarely fails. Another example – if you should be knocked down by a taxi, don't be alarmed and try to creep out from under the thing. And don't blame the driver. Apologise to him and as you are being carried away, shake hands and tell

him that while it was his cab, it was your fault. Treated in this manner, drivers are not nearly so offensive when they knock you down the next time. To attract the attention of the young lady behind a post office counter, fire a revolver three times in succession using blank cartridges. After first aid has been rendered to the attendants, step up to the counter and purchase your stamp.

The provision of refreshment for officers engaged on ceremonial duties is taken for granted in the twenty-first century. This was not the case 100 years earlier, when it was reported that 'one of the many useful pieces of work that the Christian Police Association does in connection with the London Central Police Institute, is the supply of canteens for the police when on duty on ceremonial days'. These

Police Canteens

were organised by the Rev Twentyman, who sometimes had seven or eight of these operating at one time, and they were much appreciated by the officers who used them.

In spite of this practical help given in the spirit of service, only six months later the Rev and Mrs Twentyman had to leave the service of the Association. In his farewell letter, he mentions how his stipend had been provided by personal friends of Catherine Gurney and had been guaranteed for three years. That period had now expired and owing to the change in the financial condition of the country, those friends had been unable to extend the guarantee. Under these circumstances, the ICPA Council had been compelled to ask him to terminate his engagement and seek another appointment elsewhere.

Kind words from the Council and friends around the country confirmed the fact that his three years with the Association had had a positive effect on the work.

In October 1922, Catherine faced the sudden home call of her sister-in-law Helen Gurney, the wife of Joseph John Gurney in Newcastle. An unexpected and delightful tribute to Helen was received by Catherine after visiting a police station in the county of Durham. She was being escorted to the railway station by a sergeant who, after remarking on the snow, said,

> It was just the same weather the Christmas that I had lost my wife. He saved me then and He has kept me ever since. How did He save me? Well I was as miserable as man could be. The children were cry, cry all the time. They wanted their mother, poor bairns. I had been on night duty and had no rest in the day – I had come to such a pass of misery I thought it would be best for me to be out of the world than in it – people would care more for the bairns if I wasn't there, and I was going to the station to settle up and then I thought I would go to the doc and put an end to it all. But at the station an envelope was put into my hands with my name and number on it and with best wishes for a happy Christmas and New Year. I wondered who had been sending me a letter and whoever had thought of wishing me Happy Christmas and New Year. They little knew … but when I opened it the first words that caught my eye were 'He careth for you'. I had been saying all night long 'nobody cares', but this letter said 'He careth.' Who is He? The letter soon showed me that. It was very short, but it was full of comfort. It spoke of Jesus, the friend that sticketh closer than a brother and it said, 'Casting all your care upon Him; for He careth for you.' That was personal to me and it went home to my heart. When I opened my door I found a neighbour there nursing the children and the tea all spread out by the firelight. I can tell you miss,

it quite broke me down. I just sat down in the armchair and burst into tears and then I knelt down and for the first time I thanked that Lord that he had cared for me enough to die for me. 'Who wrote the letter?' I asked, and he pulled out of his pocketbook a little folded yellowish printed paper and spread it out before me. The signature was 'Your friend, Helen Gurney'.

Less than a year later, the ICPA was mourning the loss of another stalwart, JH Tritton, who died on 11 November 1923 aged seventy-nine at his home, Lyons Hall, Great Leighs, Essex. He was originally a member of the banking firm of Barclay, Bevan, Tritton & Co which merged with others to become Barclays Bank, of which he was a director for some years. He was well known for his faith and philanthropy, taking an interest in the Association from its commencement. For over forty years he was both honorary treasurer and chairman of the Association, taking an interest in the welfare of police officers right up to the end of his life.

Before that year was over, the orphanage at Redhill had received a very important visitor. On 20 November, His Royal Highness, the Prince of Wales arrived to formally open the new chapel and the Victory Memorial School. Following an official welcome by Sir Leonard Dunning (HM Inspector of Constabulary), a member of the orphanage committee, His Royal Highness in his reply said,

> The Chairman and others have paid eloquent tributes to the founder of the orphanage, Miss Gurney. They spoke on behalf of the Force which they represented. May I add an expression of thanks on behalf of the general public? For if ever there was a work which was public spirited it is most certainly the work to which Miss Gurney has devoted so many years of her life. It must indeed be a reward to herself and her friends to see with what affection and respect they are regarded by all those who are able to appreciate the

> results that have been achieved. This orphanage, together with other admirable institutions, owes its existence entirely to this true friend of the police force.

The Police Federation was now well established and upholding the interests of officers from constable to chief inspector rank. It had therefore been decided that from January 1924 the ICPA should devote one or two pages of their monthly magazine to Federation news. With the approval of the Joint Central Committee of the Federation, it was agreed that this would take the form of extracts from the reports of the proceedings of the Central Committees and the Annual Conferences, which, it was felt, would interest the readers.

What was certainly of interest in the country at that time was the British Empire Exhibition designed to show off and promote trade from the empire countries. Although conceived in 1913, the war had put paid to development, and Government funding was not provided until 1922 when construction began at the green field site of Wembley Park in the north-west of London. The first building to be completed was Wembley Stadium and the first event was the 1923 FA Cup.

The main exhibition was officially opened by King George V on 23 April 1924, making him the first British sovereign to have words transmitted over the radio. Within the complex was a bungalow run by the Evangelical Alliance who designated 1 August as a day for the police. On that day the bungalow was placed at the disposal of the ICPA, and both prayer and evangelistic meetings were held. These meetings continued at regular intervals for the duration of the exhibition.

Following the resignation of the Rev Twentyman in 1921, there had been a gap in the administration of the Association. It was therefore a great delight when barrister Dr AB Stoney returned to the work after a ten-year absence to take up the role of honorary director and organiser. His work, under the guidance of the Holy Spirit, was to seek to revive and stimulate the spiritual work of the Association.

Dr AB Stoney

Before the end of 1925, Dr Stoney took on the additional role of editor of *OOD*. Having fulfilled the role for over forty years, Catherine Gurney no longer felt able to carry on this task. The announcement was received with nationwide regret.

To provide a proper continuity for the various works she had started, Catherine Gurney set out a trust deed which was accepted by the board of directors of the International Christian Police Trust Corporation. This deed laid a legal foundation for the International Christian Police Association, the convalescent homes and the orphanages, ensuring that they continued to be run as their foundress intended.

As time and technology marched on, the ICPA magazine reported in 1925 a new use for wireless in the fight against crime. The idea came from the fertile brain of inventor William Dubilier. He suggested that every police officer should be equipped with a small wireless set no larger than a match box. When a crime was reported to police headquarters, they would activate a blue light at all traffic controls. This would alert officers on duty that they needed to listen to their radios for an important message. In a few moments, every constable in the area would have all the facts and so the likelihood of apprehending the criminal would be greatly increased.

A new year brought more sad news. Mary (May) Griffin, who had been honorary superintendent of the Seaside Convalescent Home at Hove for over twenty years, died on New Year's Day 1926; her funeral took place on 4 January at Hove Cemetery.

May Griffin

Over forty wreaths were laid, one bearing the tribute, 'The flowers will die, but the fragrance of the life so gentle, so beautiful, so Christ-like, will last forever in the memory of the thousands who were privileged to pass through the home under her care.'

At the home's annual meeting that year was the young Chief Constable of Northampton, John Williamson, who many years later became president of the Christian Police Association. In his remarks he said,

> I have very great pleasure in travelling from Northampton today for the express purpose, and at the wish of Miss Gurney, to move this vote of thanks to the staff of this institution for their very real and very, very devoted services during the past year to the men in blue. I think it has been real true service, and when I think of the work that has been accomplished not only by this home, but the Harrogate home, I think of the hundreds of men who went into the home thinking they were going into a little purgatory, and who came away with hearts full of gratitude, full of the deep inner consciousness of what the police convalescent home really stands for.

The Annual Meeting of the ICPA was delighted to receive personal accounts of two areas of its overseas works. Miss

Helena Garratt, speaking about the work in South Africa, said:

I am so glad of this opportunity of speaking to you who are the Lord's people to ask you to pray for the work and for your comrades in South Africa.

We call ourselves the United Service Branch of the Christian Police Association. This work would never have been started except for Miss Gurney. When we went out to South Africa, we had no idea of working amongst the police, but we met Miss Gurney at a convention at Swanwick and each time I saw her during that convention, she spoke about the police of South Africa and she told me that Miss Sprigg, who had been working amongst them, had given the work up. She was greatly burdened about it, and I think it was her sadness that touched our hearts. After our arrival in South Africa, almost every mail brought us large parcels of OOD, from Miss Gurney, and I wondered what I could do with this literature. I was almost vexed at getting so much, but it stirred us up to start the work.

The first police station we visited was at Simonstown, one of the beautiful watering places of South Africa. The work is the most difficult we ever were engaged in, but we have proved the truth of the text we all know, 'There is nothing too hard for the Lord.' I am so glad to think that there is no exception to the word 'nothing', it means just what it says.

Speaking about his work in Japan, Mr RW Harris reported,

When, seven years ago, I was in South Africa, waiting for the war to end to return to England on furlough, I little knew that the Miss Garratts [sic] were to be a link in the chain that brought me into touch with the Christian Police Association, and that I should go out to Japan as its representative. After a year's furlough in England, at our farewell meeting, Miss Gurney got hold of me and asked me to consider whether the Lord was not calling me to the work of the Christian Police Mission in Tokyo. I told her I

> would pray about it. At Shanghai we received a letter from
> Mr Wilks, our Director, asking us whether we would take
> up the work in Tokyo amongst the police. Mr Wilks did
> not know that Miss Gurney had spoken to me about it in
> London, and so we took it that the Lord wanted us to do
> that work. God has blessed the work and many souls have
> been won to him.

Age and infirmity were now starting to take their toll on those valiant women who had joined Catherine Gurney in her endeavours for the police. Miss Chapman, who had started the orphanage at Harrogate with four children of police officers, was obliged to resign on health grounds after twenty-nine years' faithful service. Miss Knocker succeeded her as Lady Superintendent of St George's.

As there was now a new generation of officers since the inception of the International Christian Police Association and its associated works, there was a dearth of knowledge of its origins, what it stood for and all that Catherine Gurney and her helpers had done for the police. The honorary director, Dr Stoney, sought to rectify this by taking as many opportunities as presented themselves to address members of the Force in the stations where they served.

As Bishop Taylor Smith, former chaplain general to the Armed Forces, was unable to speak at the Annual Meeting in 1927, the organisers had persuaded Miss Christabel Pankhurst to replace him. Born in Manchester the same year as Catherine Gurney had started the Bible classes for policemen in

Christabel Pankhurst

74

her London home, Christabel, her mother, Emmeline, and sister, Sylvia were heavily involved with the women's suffrage movement in the early years of the twentieth century. While trying to disrupt a Liberal party meeting, Christabel was arrested and went to prison rather than pay the fine. She subsequently went to live in the USA, where she lectured and wrote books on the second coming of Christ.

At the Annual Meeting, she began by reminiscing about former days. 'We've worked together, haven't we?' she said.

> We've learned to know and, I hope, to respect each other. But we are now working together in a greater cause. We used to look forward to good days to come, now we are looking forward to the best day, the day of Christ's reign … The policeman has great opportunities, he is so close to the problem of sin, he is foremost in the fight, he sees its manifestation close at hand and the horror of it. He knows also the need of his own heart, face to face with tremendous temptation, he has to live the hero's life. It is good if he also knows the only one who can solve the problem of sin and evil.

During 1928 there were several reports from South Africa and Japan. Miss Huskisson, who was working in Johannesburg, noted an increase in attendance at meetings, with about 200 people at a meeting in Hope Hall, a number of whom had convalesced at The Aloes in Simonstown.

In Japan, Captain Garrard, working on behalf of the Police Missionary Union, made a priority of visiting police stations. He had 1,000 New Testaments printed and made them available to police officers who requested them. These went very quickly and he had to order another 500. Into the text they had inserted a number of topics that would be helpful to the Japanese police, and also notes on the way of salvation.

Back home, the years of selfless toil had taken their toll on Catherine Gurney, and ill health became a problem. For the first time in forty-five years, she was unable to write a New Year message in the magazine. It was also with much regret that she was unable to travel to Harrogate for the opening of the new boys' wing at St George's, the Northern Police Orphanage. On 31 May 1929, Her Royal Highness Princess Mary, Viscountess Lascelles, using a gold key supplied by the architect, opened the wing. However, it was a great delight for Catherine to be the guest of honour at the seaside convalescent home's open day on 3 July. Entertaining visitors to the home were the Brighton Police Orchestra who, in spite of being confined in the balcony, contrived to play sympathetically.

Mary Hopkinson

Miss Mary Hopkinson, the honorary secretary of the Manchester and Salford Branch, had helped Catherine Gurney from the earliest days. She had been seriously injured in 1929 when she was knocked down by a tram. Following a long period of convalescence in the Lake District, she recovered and returned to her work to public acclaim. Early in 1930 the Lord Mayor presented her with an illuminated scroll 'to commemorate the 40 years of strenuous, faithful, successful service ... devoted to the wellbeing of the widows, orphans and members of the (police) forces'. In response to this she modestly replied,

> My aim has been to carry out simply and earnestly what seemed possible, longing that anything undertaken

should be truly and faithfully done … The police and their families and all that concerns their truest welfare, have a place in my heart no words of mine can adequately express. My desire and hope is to be of service as far as possible in the time that still remains.

As the end of an era was drawing near, so came reports of Catherine Gurney's fading health. Writing in July 1930, Dr Stoney stated, 'We much regret that we cannot report any improvement in Miss Gurney's condition. She sleeps a good deal and seems much the same as last month.' It was therefore no surprise, but with a great sense of loss, when the announcement came, 'Miss Catherine Gurney, OBE entered into rest August the 11th 1930.'

Dr Stoney wrote,

Although she had been laid aside through increasing weakness for the last two years, we can hardly realise yet that we shall never see her amongst us again, full of energy and zeal for the cause of policemen and their families. Her passing is a call to those who are members of the Association to close their ranks and throw themselves heart and soul into the furtherance of the work she held so dear, and to which she gave up her life. The last time she appeared among her friends was at the reception of the Chief Constables at Hove in July 1929, when many were delighted to see her and have a kind handshake or a smile of recognition, and it was at Hove that her earthly course ended. In a quiet room, near the sea, and not far from the police home, she passed out of the shadows, and entered into the glory of the life beyond.

The funeral at Harlow Cemetery, Harrogate, followed a service at St Mary's Church conducted by the Bishop of Plymouth (a cousin of Miss Gurney) assisted by the Rev EA Chard, formerly vicar of St Mary's. Among

those present were Sir Leonard Dunning, Her Majesty's Inspector of Constabulary (HMIC), representing the Home Secretary, the trustees of the National Police Fund and the Home Office, Dr Gurney (a niece), the Mayor of Harrogate and Major General Atcherley, HMIC.

There were many tributes to Catherine Gurney.[4] From the Home Office:

> The Home Secretary [John Clynes] has learned with much regret of the death this morning of Miss Catherine Gurney, whose work as Founder of the International Christian Police Association and of the Police Convalescent Homes and Orphanages, has been of such inestimable value in furthering the welfare of police officers throughout the country, and in making provision for their orphaned children.

From the commissioner of the Metropolitan Police [Viscount Byng of Vimy]:

> We are so sorry to hear today of the death of Miss Gurney. We feel that the Metropolitan Police are losing a real friend, whose kindness and generosity over a long period of years has endeared her to all. May I extend to you all the sincere sympathy of the Force.

From the Police Federation of England and Wales:

> Practically every member of the Forces is mindful of the wonderful work accomplished by the late Miss Gurney on behalf of the Service, and her passing away

is mourned by all. In recognition of her devotion to the sick and needy, and to the children of deceased Police Officers, it is felt confidently that the Police of today will honour her memory by supporting those Institutions which she founded.

A tribute in the *Police Review:*[5]

Miss Gurney's wonderful record of service, inspired by the noblest ideals of Christian charity, and carried on the strength of a faith that never waned, in the end triumphed over all. The police of this country will surely never allow the name of Catherine Gurney to be forgotten as long as there are invalids and orphans to care for, for to her belongs the credit of founding and developing organisations, by which the force discharges its obligations to the less fortunate of their comrades, and their little ones. The best way in which the police can honour the memory of Miss Gurney is by maintaining in her spirit, the institutions which she founded for their benefit.

Miss Fry, writing from Dublin, says,

I knew Miss Gurney from almost the commencement of her work among the police, and was with her, when her mother was alive in Ladbroke Terrace. Then she came over to us here in Dublin, and enjoyed our policemen's meetings, which we had held for some time before she organised the ICPA. The meetings for the Royal Irish Constabulary and Dublin Metropolitan Police have been carried on since 1875. Miss Gurney's one great object was to win the men for Christ. That was always first, all else second.

Miss Thompson, the honorary secretary from Glasgow, writing on behalf of the Glasgow Branch says,

We most truly appreciate the wonderful work done by Miss Gurney as Foundress of the ICPA, and all her labours on behalf of the police. Her life has been a great blessing to many, and her memory will always be revered.

Miss MJ Taylor writes,

As Miss Catherine Gurney's private secretary for some years, I have had close opportunities of seeing her constant devotion and wholehearted, untiring efforts to help any member of the Police Forces, and also their wives and children. She was utterly self-sacrificing, and would go to any trouble on their behalf. Her aim was to win them for Christ and His service, and at the same time to assist them in times of ill-health or depression, and to ameliorate their often difficult lot. Her humility was remarkable. She shrank from praise or notoriety, and desired all good results to be attributed to God alone. Yet she seized on any opening to gain interest, or help, or friends for the police, or to form Bible classes for them. She opened institutes in London, Leeds, Sheffield and Cardiff, where they could obtain comfortable meals and recreation and attend Bible readings. The Christian Police Association, which she founded, has been an immense factor for good in the lives of the police all over the world, and has, no doubt, contributed to the efficiency of the force as a whole. Her motto was *put God first in everything*.

In the Annual Report of the Southern Provincial Police School of 1928 is one of the last written messages from Catherine Gurney.

We cannot look back over the 45 years of our orphanage and convalescent home life without deep and earnest thanksgiving to our Heavenly Father for the guidance vouchsafed us from day to day and for the constant supply of all our needs (spiritual and temporal) so long as we followed His bidding. How often have we proved the old saying that 'God's biddings are enablings!'

It is not what *seems* but what *is* that matters. The

waves may be rushing and roaring in front and the enemy gathering its army against Israel behind, fermenting discontent and distrust of God, but simple definite obedience paves the way for miracle. The Word is clear, go forward! And though thousands might say impossible, that could not change God's plain command. With Him nothing is impossible, and if we will only trust Him, He will show us the way out of every difficulty. In simple language we are told (Proverbs 3:5–6), 'Trust in the Lord with all thine heart; and lean not unto thine own understanding. In all thy ways acknowledge him, and he shall direct thy paths.' Therefore, let us obediently, steadily, and cheerfully

GO FORWARD!

C Gurney

Beautiful life is that whose span
Is spent in service for God and man,
Forgetting self in all that it can.[6]

Chapter 5

The death of Catherine Gurney was a pivotal point for all five of the works that she had started for the benefit of the police. Her strong personality, her unswerving faith and her seemingly indomitable spirit had all contributed to the birth and growth of the ICPA, the orphanages and the convalescent homes. In an era of great Christian philanthropy, she had used her network of contacts to the greatest possible advantage. But things were about to change. In fact, circumstances demanded that change was essential if the works were to continue and flourish.

The Great War (1914–18) had not only taken its toll of hundreds of thousands of lives, but also had seriously affected the economies of the countries involved. Recession led to the Great Depression of 1929–32 and no one was immune from its effects. This was also a time when many of those stalwarts who had assisted in the founding of Miss Gurney's works were reaching old age and incapacity.

Although gone, she was not forgotten. On Christmas Eve 1930, about fifteen officers convalescing at St Andrew's, the Northern Police Convalescent Home, visited her grave at Harlow Hill Cemetery to lay a holly cross on it. There they found that others had visited before them to lay tokens of remembrance. The stone around the grave had now been

LAST RESTING-PLACE.

completed and bore the inscription 'In loving memory of Catherine Gurney, foundress of the International Christian Police Association. "His servants shall serve him and they shall see his face."'

Early 1931 saw the death of another ICPA pioneer, Emma Garratt, who, with Catherine Gurney's encouragement, had started the work in South Africa assisted by her sisters, May and Helena. She was buried in Dido Valley Cemetery, Glencairn.

Thankfully, the Great Depression did not slow down or halt the quest for new ways to fight crime. Dr Edmond Locard, director of the Police Laboratories at Lyon, France, had discovered that a minute examination of dust, hairs, tobacco ash, etc was an invaluable aid in the detection of criminals. A study of what he called 'professional dusts' showed that evidence of someone's occupation may be retained in their ears, nostrils and clothes for as long as two years. One particular case study concerned several men, known to be associates, who had been caught with counterfeit coins. It was suspected that they had been involved in the manufacture of the coins and so their clothes were carefully brushed and the dust chemically examined. It turned out to contain pyroantimonate of sodium, tin salts and a large amount of lead. This proved their association and involvement in the coins' manufacture beyond doubt, and they were convicted.

There was, however, nothing counterfeit about the work

of Dr AB Stoney, the barrister who had worked with Catherine Gurney for over forty years. His wife, too, had been involved with the work in a variety of ways, including covering for the honorary superintendents of both convalescent homes during summer absences. In recognition of such dedicated service, the couple were presented with an illuminated address and a number of gifts at a gathering of his old friends on 8 July 1931.

It was a real shock to the Association when, less than a year later, on 14 April 1932, Dr Stoney died suddenly at the age of eighty-one. Originally from Rathlahine, County Clare in Ireland, Arbuthnot Butler Stoney had been involved with the Association since its inception at Resington Lodge, Kensington. For family reasons he had spent some time in both Ireland and Canada, but had always kept in touch with the work. Loyal to the memory of Catherine Gurney, his great desire was to keep the different institutions in touch with each other, and to see that the objects for which they were established were maintained.

Captain Raymond Tyler

Of course, the passing of Dr Stoney left a large gap in the organisation, and one that the ICPA Council was eager to fill at the earliest opportunity. Fast approaching was the fiftieth anniversary of the founding of the ICPA and 1933 saw the appointment of a new honorary director. Raymond Tyler, a retired captain in the RAF, came from Leicestershire to take up the appointment. He was reported to be 'in every way qualified for the work'.

Royal patronage was not new, but it was a lovely

surprise when at noon on 3 January 1933, St George's, the Northern Police Orphanage, received a phone call from Harewood House. Her Royal Highness the Princess Royal would be paying an informal visit with her two sons at about 5pm. This caused much excitement, and on her arrival, the children were keen to show her the toys they had received. The royal party stayed until nearly 7pm, leaving a very happy atmosphere behind them.

A stone-laying ceremony took place later that year at St Andrew's, Harrogate, to mark the official commencement of work on the Gurney Memorial Wing. Dr Nimmo Watson, who had voluntarily given his services to the police for the previous thirty years, performed the ceremony which was attended by the Mayor and Mayoress of Harrogate, and the chief constables of Bradford, Durham, Gateshead, Halifax, Lancashire, Manchester and the West Riding of Yorkshire. It was astounding to note that during those previous thirty years, over 11,000 patients passed through the home. The new wing was due to be officially opened in February 1934.

While things were looking bright at the convalescent home, it was a much darker outlook on the other side of the Pennines. At the British Union of Fascists meeting in the Free Trade Hall in Manchester, chaos and rioting erupted due to the presence of anti-fascist communists. The police were called and had to break up the fighting between the two sides. We need to remember also that it was the year that Adolf Hitler had become Chancellor of Germany and dark tales were beginning to emerge from Europe.

In spite of the gloomy accounts of law-breaking, innovation was still alive and well in UK policing. We sometimes think that volunteers working alongside the police is a new thing, but by the end of 1933 the Chief Constable of Gravesend in Kent had made arrangements for the owners of fast cars in his area to place them at his disposal in the event of an emergency. He appointed them as 'special motor constables' and they were contacted by telephone if no police cars were available. In particular, they were formed to cope with 'motor bandits'. It is tempting to think that his inspiration may have come from tales of car chases involving Bonnie Parker and Clyde Barrow in the USA.

Although the deaths of Bonnie and Clyde in 1934 were mourned by few, there was a certain band of women in the UK whose passing was to have a much greater effect on the work of the ICPA.

Almost every edition of the magazine between 1932 and 1934 contained an obituary of some faithful Christian woman who had been instrumental in starting ICPA groups in her town or city. These were the determined ladies who had been there at the start of things, and had done so much to keep the Association alive during and after the First World War when many branches had been decimated.

During this period, the Chief Constable of Portsmouth, Thomas Davies, wrote to the ICPA headquarters commenting on the needs of the day.

> Probably at no previous time in history has this world of ours been more in need of Christianity than it is today; the international atmosphere is full of such unrest as to fill one with grave forebodings as to the future; at home we have the grey clouds of depression through which, happily, faint rays of sunshine are now commencing to disperse. But apart from this general and pressing need of faith it has been increasingly borne upon me, during my many years of service [he served as Chief Constable for 33 years from 1907], that a true Christian outlook is as essential to a police officer in the complete discharge of his public work as is a sound knowledge of his duties and powers. These two attributes walk hand in hand – mutually reliant

and comprising together all that is required to make the
perfect policeman; just as by the latter he knows *what to do*
so by the former he knows *how to do it*; there is no question
of their relative importance – they are inseparable. Let
us never forget that the police service of a country is the
hallmark of its civilisation, which, in its highest sense, is
Christianity and all the great and noble things which that
word conveys.

Further change in the ICPA was to take place before the end
of 1934. Unlike the convalescent homes and orphanages, the
Police Institute in Central London which housed the ICPA
headquarters, was in rented property, and its maintenance
over the years had led to heavy financial loss. The Council
of the Association felt that it was right to move to smaller
offices where future requirements could be assessed, subject
to the necessary funds being available.

Thankfully, a suite of rooms was rented at 117 Victoria
Street, Westminster. Although they would no longer be able
to offer sleeping accommodation or restaurant facilities,
there would still be a lounge available during the week
which would be used on Sundays for afternoon tea and a
short service.

For a few months, things seemed to settle down, which
was probably just as well, as July 1935 saw the review of
the Police Forces by King George V in Hyde Park, as part
of the Silver Jubilee celebrations. Several thousand police
officers from England, Wales and Scotland descended
on London for the event and considered it a privilege to
parade before the King and Queen. There should have
been 300 officers from the Royal Ulster Constabulary in
the march past, but they were prevented from attending
due to disturbances in Belfast.

Internationally, another event took place that year which has had a profound effect on one area of work that was dear to Catherine Gurney's heart. Alcoholism had been a real problem in the late nineteenth and early twentieth centuries, with many movements set up to encourage men and women to  pledge themselves to total abstinence from alcohol. Even the era of prohibition in the USA had not eradicated the problem. It is said that when Bill Wilson met Dr Bob Smith in Akron, Ohio, an acorn was planted out of which has grown the mighty oak of Alcoholics Anonymous. Together with early members of their first self-help group, Bill Wilson and Dr Bob developed a programme of spiritual and character development which has come to be known as 'The twelve steps'. Still today Alcoholics Anonymous groups around the world seek to stay sober and help other alcoholics achieve sobriety. With very clear Christian roots, they continue to encourage members to find that 'higher power' that will help them conquer their addiction.

It is hardly surprising that men and women who feel called by God into a particular sphere of service often throw themselves into the work with such passion and effort that their health suffers. The ICPA was not immune to this, and it was with great regret that after such a short time, Captain Tyler was obliged to relinquish his post as honorary director on doctor's orders.

With a move to new headquarters and a funding crisis, the Council did not want to leave the ship without a rudder, so to speak, for too long, and so appointed a new director in January 1936.

George Paisley

George Paisley came to the ICPA from the North East India General Mission and was to be in post for twenty-three years. He grew up in Dublin where his father worked with Miss Fry, caring for the spiritual welfare of the men of the Dublin Metropolitan Police and the Royal Irish Constabulary. After serving in the South Irish Horse (a territorial yeomanry of the British Army) during the First World War, he obtained a commission in the Indian Army, but he did not find any spiritual satisfaction in life until September 1925, when he responded to the call of God during a gospel meeting.

Over the years, Catherine Gurney's work had often received royal patronage and so it was a shock, not only to the country, but also to the ICPA in particular, when King George V died at the end of January 1936. He had been patron of both convalescent homes and both orphanages. Sympathy was expressed to Queen Mary and the Royal Family.

The New Year's Honours List that year had included the name of one prominent ICPA member, John Williamson. Having been appointed Chief Constable of Northampton at the age of thirty-three, he had now held the position for twelve years. Apart from his work with the Chief Constables' Association, he was also a member of the governing body of the Redhill police orphanage, a director of the Christian Police Trust Corporation Ltd and a member of the Council of the ICPA. He was awarded the OBE for his contribution to policing.

CHIEF CONSTABLE MADE AN O.B.E.

MR. J. WILLIAMSON (Northampton).

John Williamson

It is often thought that use of the term 'Police Service' is something comparatively recent. However, *The Times* reported on the annual ICPA meetings and in quoting John Williamson who had chaired the meeting, said 'he used the term service rather than force, because they were no longer the force, as they were known in the old days, but a service to serve their neighbours as well as to look after the enemies of society'.[7]

A service, of course, was not a new concept to those who had been approached and responded to the challenges set by Catherine Gurney. Service to both king and country, without fear or favour, was the duty of every police officer, and so it must have caused some consternation in the ranks when the one whom they had sworn to serve declined to take upon himself the duty he had inherited. King Edward VIII abdicated in 1936. He had been proclaimed king on the death of his father but had not been officially crowned. This not only caused uproar in the Government of the day but led to much heartache and bitterness within the Royal Family. It fell to his younger brother, Prince Albert, Duke of York, to take up the call, and he was crowned King George VI in Westminster Abbey on 12 May 1937. The ICPA magazine carried an informal picture of the King and Queen Elizabeth with their daughters, the Princesses Elizabeth and Margaret.

There had been some correspondence at the ICPA headquarters concerning the content of the magazine. Apparently some thought that it would better serve the needs of the police if there was more non-Christian content.

Honorary director George Paisley's response had first of all been to declare in an editorial that as a Christian organisation that would be the priority for content. Secondly, he started a series of articles entitled, 'Can a Policeman be a Christian?' These were personal accounts from officers across the UK, the first from Chief Inspector Reginald Morrish of the Metropolitan Police. Subsequent issues related the stories of Constable J Bold of the Royal Ulster Constabulary, Constables George Parkinson from Aberdeen and William Laws from Carlisle. Also in the series was an article from John Williamson, OBE, Chief Constable of Northampton. All of these men gave a clear and concise account of their own faith and affirmed in the strongest possible way that they had found it possible to be both a committed Christian and a police officer.

Towards the end of the series, Constable Stan Harrison of the Metropolitan Police wrote,

> A policeman needs to be a Christian because he has so many decisions to make, advice and assistance to give, that he cannot expect to do it in his own strength; he needs the guidance of one who is all powerful, all wise and understanding. King Solomon, said to be the wisest man who ever lived, realised this need, and describing himself as a little child, prayed thus: 'Give therefore thy servant an understanding heart to judge thy people, that I may discern between good and bad' (1 Kings 3 v 9).

It really was a period of rapid change in a number of areas of Catherine Gurney's ministry. In the north of the country, those at St George's, the Northern Police Orphanage, were mourning the loss of their first superintendent, Miss Emma Chapman, who had died at the end of 1936. Across the field at St Andrew's, the Northern Convalescent Home, they were saddened by the passing of Mr JH Wardman, a former sergeant in the West Riding Constabulary who, following his retirement from the Force, had served for eighteen years as a steward at the home.

Meanwhile, in the south of the country, the staff and patients at the Southern Convalescent Home were rejoicing at the installation of an electric lift. No longer would they have to see men with broken limbs and weak hearts making their agonisingly slow progress up the stairs. They were also thankful that they had escaped the scarlet fever epidemic which had swept the country, claiming many lives.

Back in London there was more change at the ICPA headquarters. Miss Hall, who had been secretary of the Association for eight years, had tendered her resignation but was soon replaced by Miss Ruth Harris. Before another six months had passed, the office was on the move again, this time just a short distance from Victoria Street to Denison House, 296 Vauxhall Bridge Road. Apart from a temporary move, it was due to stay here for a good number of years.

Always trying to reflect current affairs, the ICPA magazine carried an article by FW Pitt on events in Europe. He said,

> The complete swallowing up of one great European state by another must have made the plans and policies of statesmen look ridiculous even in their own eyes. Everyone knew there would be a clash between Germany and Austria, and perhaps a suzerainty or a war, but we venture to think that no-one but Hitler and Mussolini ever thought that Austria would be wiped off the map in a night without firing a shot. Nor would they had there not been deliberate lying and deception to keep Britain and France from knowing what was going on between Hitler and Mussolini. Our Government was actually arranging

talks with the dictators with a view to the settlement of difficulties when the Vienna bombshell shattered our complacent belief in the moral integrity of the Fuehrer and the Duce. It is now clear that these two tyrants had agreed between themselves to assist each other to obtain Austria for the one and Spain for the other.

Change was in the air at Harrogate when the Lady Superintendent, Miss Thompson, was forced to retire on doctor's orders so that she might lead a less exertive life. A tribute from those who worked with her appeared in the ICPA magazine:

> To have been, during so long a period, an understanding friend and wise counsellor to thousands of convalescent policemen, to have made St Andrews by her gracious and motherly presence into a real home, to have radiated an atmosphere of peace and happiness all around her and to have sent scores of patients back to their own homes with a new outlook on life and with new spiritual aspirations, is a work of which any woman might be justly proud. But Miss Thompson disclaims any praise for such achievement, ascribing it all to the goodness and grace of God alone. Those of us who have had the privilege of working with Miss Thompson would like to pay tribute to her wise and able leadership, her large-hearted friendship and her wonderful thoughtfulness for others. She has a special gift for initiating beginners into new work and her keen appreciation of each individual contribution of service ever calls out the best. 'I hope that you will be happy at St Andrews,' wrote Miss Gurney when I [a fellow worker] was about to join the staff here, but no-one could fail to be happy with Miss Thompson.

At the annual meeting of the Northern Convalescent Home the following year, it was recorded that

In addition to the Committee on the platform were Miss Thompson, who for 32 years had been Lady Superintendent of the Convalescent Home, and Sister Carlisle, who for 18 years had been Sister in Charge at the Home. In the name of the Northern Forces of England and Wales and the City of Glasgow, the

Miss Thompson

President presented Miss Thompson with an illuminated address from the Committee and a cheque for £229 4s 11d from the Northern Forces, and to Sister Carlisle was given a cheque for £202 16s 11d. In presenting the cheques, Sir William Ingilby referred to the very deep appreciation that the members of the Northern Forces felt for all Miss Thompson had done for them and for the regard in which they held her; he referred also to the untiring devotion and help that Sister Carlisle had given to the members of the Forces who had come sick and sorry for themselves to the Home.

Changes at Harrogate would pale into insignificance when compared to what was happening elsewhere. With the situation in Europe deteriorating, the country was starting to prepare for anticipated hostilities. At the Northern Police Orphanage, the whole household retired to bed at 6pm one night, only to be aroused shortly after by a prearranged signal to take the place of an air raid warning. Everyone rose in silence, dressed as speedily as possible and were within the allotted rooms in four minutes. However, everyone had been fully awake and on tenterhooks for the first sound of the signal.

After all negotiations, warnings and threats had been ignored by the Nazi regime, the UK and its empire was once again plunged into war as declared by Prime Minister Neville Chamberlain on 3 September 1939. This would be a challenging time for the ICPA, with many of its members conscripted into the armed services, just as in the earlier conflict from 1914 to 1918. But there would be the additional challenge of reaching out to the thousands of War Reserves and Special Constables. It was important in those dark days to try to keep as upbeat as possible and in spite of the constraints of the war, there were many encouraging articles in the ICPA magazine, one of which was a tribute to Mary Hopkinson, celebrating the Golden Jubilee of the Manchester and Salford Police and Fire Brigade's Orphanage and Benevolent Fund:

> Many readers of *On and Off Duty* during the last 54 years will be acquainted with the name of Miss Hopkinson as Honorary Secretary of the Manchester and Salford Branch of the ICPA in which she has performed a great work for the spiritual life of these forces and fire brigades, to which may be added the Manchester Division of Lancashire and the Altrincham Division of Cheshire Constabularies. This has been but one of her activities in connection with the police and fire brigades for which all concerned are greatly indebted to her.
>
> In 1889 Miss Hopkinson, having learnt much of the police and their families during four happy years in connection with the ICPA, was encouraged by Miss Gurney to organise a scheme for the benefit of widows and fatherless children of the forces, and very soon under the wise guidance and help of her father, Alderman Hopkinson of Manchester, and friends, the Manchester and Salford Police and Fire Brigade's Orphanage and Benevolent Fund was established.
>
> It is therefore fitting that such a Jubilee should not be allowed to pass without tribute being paid to her long and loving service. It is due to Miss Hopkinson's seemingly unlimited capacity and indefatigable energy that the Fund

has flourished and been so successfully administered.

Her visitation during all kinds of weather to the needy, distressed and bereaved, her patience and deep understanding of humanity and attention to detail has time and again seemed phenomenal. By the exercise of those qualities she has throughout those fifty years brought peace, comfort and joy to many bereft of husband and father, and revealed to them the silver lining through the dark clouds of distress and sorrow.

Following the Battle of Britain in 1940 and the Blitz which followed, the ICPA Council decided that it was no longer safe to run the Association from central London. Therefore, as a temporary measure, the office was moved to George Paisley's home at Shalem, 36 Lordsbury Field, Wallington, Surrey.

Wallington was close to several Royal Air Force fighter bases and so the area was a target for air raids. In February 1941, George Paisley wrote, 'It is not a new experience for us to be occupied with the preparation of our magazine during an air raid. It has happened before and no doubt will happen again, but the fact of living so close to the edge of eternity in these days is always with us.'

For some, those years were to herald a passing into the eternity that George Paisley mentioned. Among them were several who had served well in the works started by Catherine Gurney. Captain Murray Barclay Buxton, who for many years had been the chairman of the Christian Police Trust Corporation, was killed as the result of enemy action. Mr H Gale, a member of the ICPA Council, who had the welfare of the police very much at heart, also died. But not least was the passing of Mrs Agnes Dovey (neé Campbell) in 1941.

As a single woman, Agnes Campbell had been converted during a mission held by Messrs Moody and Sankey in

Glasgow. She had accompanied Catherine Gurney to a meeting held at the Police Office, Albion Street in 1884 by kind permission of the chief constable, Captain McAll. In November that year, the Glasgow Branch of the ICPA was launched at the Christian Institute in Bothwell Street. Miss Campbell was appointed honorary secretary and treasurer.

The work grew and was established in many police divisions. Agnes Campbell also travelled to many parts of Scotland, visiting police stations and opening new branches. Throughout her life she always had the spiritual welfare of the police at heart, and even when she settled in Edinburgh she always tried to return to Glasgow for their Annual Meetings.

The war had cut right across organised life and activity, so it seemed that the ICPA was in an impossible situation. Many subscribers to the work had been lost and not totally replaced. There were severe financial constraints which led to constant appeals, but the work did continue, and in spite of the situation, Christians in the police maintained a strong witness to their faith. However, the only branches that continued to operate normally were Glasgow, Manchester and Northampton.

The necessities of the war effort affected just about everybody. The Southern Provincial Police Orphanage and School at Redhill had taken in some of the children evacuated from the London area. Although there were some air raids in the vicinity, it was reported that none of the buildings were damaged and none of the children had any frightening experiences. Some of the boys helped the gardener with the 'Dig for Victory' campaign, and the pigs they had been rearing supplemented the meat ration.

By the middle of 1941, the ICPA faced another stricture. The printers had been able to keep up the supply of paper until then, but in spite of an endorsement from the Chief Constables' Association that *OOD* should be classified as 'a paper of value to an essential service', the number of pages had to be reduced.

At Harrogate, the Northern Police Convalescent Home opened an extension housing seven new bedrooms. This timely event benefited many police officers who had been injured in the air raids. Across the field at the Northern Police Orphanage, they received reports of a number of old boys who were now serving in HM Forces, some of them already overseas. A number of the girls had also volunteered and were serving as wardens, nurses or in other women's services.

Madeleine Kerr, who had given many years of loyal service as superintendent of the Police Seaside Home at Hove, was awarded the MBE in the King's Birthday Honours of 1942.

In that same year, due to enemy action over London it was decided that the Annual Meeting of the ICPA should be held in Northampton. In spite of the war, delegates came from Birmingham, Glasgow, Leicester, Liverpool, London, Manchester and Northampton.

Change was also afoot at the Northern Police Orphanage at Harrogate. The Annual General Meeting of their Council had unanimously decided that it was time to change the name. Following their application to the Charity Commissioners for a scheme which would allow them to do this, they were delighted to receive the news that from 18 September 1942 the Northern Police Orphanage should henceforth be known as St George's House.

In June 1943 when the Keswick Convention was held in Portstewart, County Londonderry, there were eighteen

Christian police officers present. During the course of the convention, they held a meeting to discuss the possibility of forming a branch of the ICPA that would encompass all six counties of Northern Ireland. Head Constable Cowan from Bangor was appointed the honorary secretary, and it was decided that they would send out a monthly newsletter to all Christians in the Royal Ulster Constabulary, and eventually to circulate a copy of the magazine *OOD* to every police station.

Barely two months later on 11 August, the thirteenth anniversary of the death of Catherine Gurney, her cousin Jessie Margaret Tritton also passed away. She had been a stalwart of the work, being honorary secretary of the Southern Branch of the ICPA when it began and arranging meetings across a large part of south London. When the Police Institute was started, she was one of the pioneer helpers, and from 1888 to 1936 she had been the honorary secretary of the Police Missionary Union. Following the death of Catherine Gurney, Miss Tritton had compiled the tribute booklet, *A Beloved Lady*.

Five and half years of war in Europe finally came to an end in 1945. It had been an extremely difficult time for the ICPA, but the work had been able to continue and the adverse circumstances were a spur, encouraging officers to hold meetings in new locations throughout the country with good and lasting results. During those war years, 131 new members joined the Association at home and overseas.

But the Council of the ICPA were not content to sit back and take things easy. They formulated plans to visit existing branches and establish new ones, communicate with existing members to encourage them in their Christian life and conduct, encouraging and furthering evangelical witness in the police, and seeking some general recognition by the Home Office on proposals by the ICPA concerning the spiritual needs of the Police Service. This latter desire would not be fulfilled for many years.

The arrival of peace brought with it another change in the leadership of the ICPA. The chairman of the Council, Lieutenant Colonel DCD Munro, DSO, MC, had announced his retirement from the post and the vice-chairman, Mr John Williamson, OBE, Chief Constable of Northampton, had been appointed to replace him. This appointment was hugely welcomed as John Williamson was the first serving police officer to become chairman.

Change was also in the air at the Police Seaside Convalescent Home at Hove. Madeleine Kerr, the superintendent since 1926, had announced her retirement. On relinquishing her work she wrote,

> I feel that now the war is over, there are many younger and stronger women more fitted to filling my place here ... I take away with me glad remembrances and – especially through the grim years of war – a deep pride in and admiration for the men in blue, who never failed to make a heroic stand in their unutterably fierce trial.

You could never be sure where the work of the ICPA was going to crop up next. In her lifetime, Catherine Gurney had sought to encourage care for the police at home and overseas, sometimes through her presence and elsewhere by encouraging others to spread the message. Early in 1946 a report was received from PC Reindorf Sereboo of the Gold Coast Police Branch of the ICPA – known today as Ghana – rejoicing that the branch was very active. Monthly meetings were being held and morning services conducted four times a week. They were also praying that police officers in other parts of West Africa would be able to join the organisation in due course.

Back in the UK, times were still hard and food rationing still in place, but colonial ties and the bond of policing remained strong. In the state of Victoria, Australia, the police wanted to do something practical to help their colleagues on the other side of the world, and came up with the idea of sending food parcels. With the wholehearted support of Alex Duncan, a former chief inspector at New Scotland Yard and then Chief Commissioner of Police in Victoria, the scheme got underway. The parcels, each weighing about 7lb, contained tinned steak and vegetables, preserved fruit, cheese, dripping, jelly crystals, powdered milk, custard powder and honey. Whilst some UK families were adopted by individuals or groups at police stations, others contributed to the scheme by way of regular deductions from their salaries.

Long after the end of the war the financial position of the ICPA remained a concern. Office rent and printing costs had risen and expenses generally had increased. Despite best efforts to keep costs down, for seven years there had been an excess of expenditure over income and the ICPA was having to draw extensively on its invested funds. But the Council were not downhearted and looked to expand the work.

One part of Catherine Gurney's work was not progressing at that time. There had been a change in social care policy and it was no longer considered beneficial to remove children from their homes when one parent died. As a result, fewer and fewer children were coming into the Southern Provincial Police School at Redhill and it finally closed in 1947, with the premises being sold in 1948. However, the vision for caring for the bereaved children of police officers was not dimmed. The capital realised from the sale of the Redhill property was invested and became known as The Gurney Fund. Subsequently, the original foundation stone was recovered from the site and relocated to the Fund's headquarters at Worthing in Sussex. It read:

> *To the glory of God.*
> *In memory of Her Most*
> *Gracious Majesty*
> *Queen Victoria*
> *and for the benefit of the*
> *fatherless children of the police,*
> *this stone was laid by*
> *The Countess of Chichester,*
> *July 3rd 1901.*
> *Bless the Lord O my soul and forget*
> *not all His Benefits. Psalm CIII.2*
> *Spencer Grant Architects, C. B. Roberts & Co. Builder*

Since the beginning of 1947, the Council of the ICPA had been looking at the possibility of appointing a missioner for the Metropolitan Police. They had approached the London City Mission (LCM) with the idea as they already had a missioner working with the City of London Police. While the LCM supported the proposal and would have been happy to appoint someone for the task, they insisted that the ICPA be responsible for providing half of the man's salary. This was not going to be an easy task, given the precarious state of ICPA finances, but they decided to press on.

With much joy, Mr EFM Barnard was appointed as Missioner to the Police in the London area from 1 December 1947. A retired Naval architect, Mr Barnard was well used to working in a male environment and had come to the post highly recommended. Sadly, he was only able to serve in the post for two years as he passed away suddenly in November 1949. It was said that during his time as missioner he personally contacted nearly 5,000 men and women in the police, who held him in high esteem.

That same year, the *Church of England Newspaper* of 15 August[8] reported comments made by HRH Princess Elizabeth when addressing a Christian youth organisation. She said,

Princess Elizabeth

> We are commissioned to be witnesses to the truth of the Gospel of our Lord Jesus Christ. A witness is one who speaks of that which he knows about at first hand. We need to have a knowledge of our faith that we can be bold in our witness and adventurous in our living. We know that we shall probably be in a minority wherever we are. We know we shall have to face insecurity, opposition, and perhaps danger, for the confession of our faith. But the Christian Church has always prospered in adversity, and we must certainly not be afraid. I think it is comforting to remember those wonderful marching orders, given by Joshua: 'Be strong and of good courage,' and then to think of the other men and women in times past who, through the grace of God, were enabled to go forward into an unknown future with confidence and with resolve.

One person who certainly needed to 'be strong and of good courage' that year was John Williamson, Chief Constable of Northampton and chairman of the ICPA Council. He and his wife were returning from holiday on 5 September when their car overturned near Carlisle. Both of them were seriously injured, and sadly Mrs Williamson passed away three days later.

With the loss and hardship that the war had brought

and the austerity measures that were needed afterwards to get the nation back on its feet, something was required to bring about a feel-good factor, if only for a short while. As 1947 was drawing to a close there was indeed something to celebrate. On 20 November, Princess Elizabeth (later to be Queen Elizabeth II) married Prince Philip at Westminster Abbey. The crowds cheered, and the nation rejoiced with the young couple as they embarked on their new life together.

In the life of the ICPA it would be another eighteen months before *OOD* celebrated a 'first' – the first published testimony of a female member of the police. It was the story of Florence Brock, a sergeant in the Royal Ulster Constabulary who had been brought up to go to church but never made a profession of faith in God. In June 1948 she was on temporary transfer to Bangor, County Down when she started having conversations with a Christian police officer. As a result, she went with him to a minister and, kneeling down with both men, she accepted Jesus Christ as her own personal Saviour.

Chapter 6

George Dixon

There are many people who still refer to the good old days of policing as the *Dixon of Dock Green* era. It was a time when police officers in towns and cities had small beats to patrol, and were able to gain intimate knowledge of the residents and what was going on in their area. The term '*Dixon of Dock Green*' comes from the title of a BBC television programme shown from 1955 to 1976 but the central character, PC George Dixon, was first portrayed in a film called *The Blue Lamp* which was released in 1950. In the film, George Dixon is soon to retire but attends the scene of a robbery where he confronts the perpetrator who is armed, resulting in the police officer being shot and killed; the criminal was later arrested. The officer's character was subsequently resurrected to make the TV series.

Life for the ordinary person in the UK was still difficult. There was much rebuilding to be done after the war and rationing for most goods was still in force. However, for the motorist there was some relief as wartime rationing of petrol was lifted in 1950. It must be noted, of course, that in those days only one in seven families owned a car!

To try to provide a tonic for the nation, the Festival of Britain was organised. The principal exhibition was on the South Bank site of the River Thames, near Waterloo, but other exhibitions took place around London and the rest of Britain. It was also a celebration of the centenary of the Great Exhibition of 1851.

Opened by King George VI on 3 May, it ran for five months through to September 1951. During the final month, another event took place on the opposite side of the river. Organised by the World's Evangelical Alliance, a united exhibition and evangelical campaign took place in Westminster Central Hall. The central feature of the exhibition was a special display of all the first editions of the English Bible which had been loaned for the occasion. The ICPA was one of the organisations represented.

Those attending were greeted, as they passed through the doors, by a written message from Queen Elizabeth:

> I am most happy to send my good wishes for the success of the exhibition which the World's Evangelical Alliance has arranged for this festival year, together with my congratulations on maintaining the vision and enterprise which had always been a characteristic of the Alliance for more than 100 years, and which find a worthy expression today.
>
> That cherished inheritance which we call the British way of life has its source and inspiration in the great ideals of Christianity. It is fitting, indeed, that we should take this opportunity of showing how the life of our nation has long been influenced by our faith, and moulded by the Bible. I can truly say that the King and I long to see the Bible back where it ought to be, as a guide and comfort in the homes and lives of our people. From our own experience, we know what the Bible can mean for personal life.

> I hope this exhibition will help our nation to be
> Christian in fact as well as in name, and so to play its full
> part in leading the world towards righteousness and peace.
> Elizabeth R

While this was happening in London, the ICPA branch in Northern Ireland was holding a gospel event in the town hall at Portrush from 8 to 15 September. Delegates from England, Ireland, Scotland and Wales led the campaign, waging war against the forces of evil.

Shortly after the meetings in Portrush, the Chairman of Council, John Williamson, Chief Constable of Northampton, was privileged to give the message at a midweek service broadcast for the BBC Midland region. The text of the message was subsequently turned into a tract called 'Why I believe in Christ', which was widely distributed by the ICPA.

Some years seemed to bring more sad news than glad news and 1952 was one of them. The year opened with the news that Mary Hopkinson had passed away in the previous December, and among many tributes made to her untiring efforts on behalf of police officers and their families was the following:

> It is over 60 years since that gracious lady made her name synonymous with that of the Manchester and Salford Branch of the ICPA. She would have made no claim that she was instrumental in the inauguration of the Association, that privilege she always insisted was Miss Gurney's. It can be claimed, on her behalf, however, that she not only started the Manchester and Salford Branch and inspired it throughout her life, but she also exercised a tremendous influence on the Association as a whole.
>
> One hesitates to mention how she showed her great affection for the police and her real concern for their problems. She would have shunned such recognition, but

we owe it to her, and to God, to remind ourselves whenst came these things.

Miss Hopkinson's predominant concern was for the spiritual wellbeing of the police and for their families and it was to that end she started the Manchester Branch of the ICPA and tended it with such tireless devotion. It was her kindness of heart, her tenderness of sympathy and her thoughtfulness which caused her to visit the sick members of the Manchester and Salford police and fire brigades and their families regularly until only a few years ago, and to establish by her own and other private financial help, the Manchester and Salford Police and Fire Brigade's Benevolent Fund to afford assistance to the families of deceased police officers and firemen. Nor was her interest confined to Manchester and Salford, for she often visited neighbouring Police Forces, and sent them her customary Christmas letter.

Having been thrust into the monarchy, overcome a serious speech impediment, and survived the Second World War, it was with great sadness that the nation learned of the death of King George VI on 6 February 1952 at the age of fifty-six. This, of course, meant that the 25-year-old Princess Elizabeth became Queen Elizabeth II.

More sad news was to come with the announcement of the death of Miss Evelyn Knocker on 27 May. She had been Lady Superintendent of St George's House, Harrogate, providing dedicated service to the children of police officers from 1926 until her retirement in 1949. Being around six feet

Evelyn Knocker

tall and wearing size twelve shoes, she must have appeared a formidable figure to the small children in her care. With remarkable management and organisational skills she was able to run the house, which normally had about seventy children of both sexes from preschool age up to about seventeen years.

Thankfully, it was not all doom and gloom, as *OOD* continued to publish news of its members around the country. Under the heading 'A Wedding has been Arranged', the July/August edition reported, 'We are happy to announce the engagement between Ronald Perrett, "A" Division Metropolitan Police, and Olive Schooling of South Petherton, Somerset.' Ron was widely known for his faith and led many Christian police witness teams around the country both as a serving officer and later in retirement.

Bearing witness to one's faith had always been part of the ICPA ethos and many members had been asking if it was possible to have a buttonhole or pin badge to show their allegiance. Finally, towards the end of 1952, ICPA member Harold Neaves of the Metropolitan Police designed a badge that was felt to embody all that the Association  stood for. Based on a shield, the top portion was gold and the bottom blue. In heraldry, these two colours used together signify truth and confidence. In the centre was an open book to denote the centrality of the Word of God. The cross, coloured red, represented the sacrificial life and death of the Lord Jesus Christ. The initials of the Association were placed on top of the book, within the arms of the cross. Members were encouraged to wear the badge as a means of identification with other ICPA members and a witness to their colleagues.

The following year was one of real anticipation in many ways. The most prominent event was to take place in Westminster Abbey in June with the coronation of Queen Elizabeth II. In May, New Zealand mountaineer Edmund Hillary, with the help of Sherpa mountaineer Tenzing Norgay, conquered Mount Everest. That same year, James Watson and Francis Crick discovered the structure of DNA.

With such remarkable things happening, you could be forgiven for thinking that the Annual Report of the ICPA would be overlooked. But within the report was the following little golden nugget of news.

> About 70 years ago, God in His wisdom, raised up three ladies, ladies of refinement and culture … The names of Miss Elise Sandes, Miss Agnes Weston and Miss Catherine Gurney were household names. Not so today. A generation has arisen that know not these three great women. Nevertheless, the work began by Miss Sandes among the soldiers, by Miss Weston among sailors and by Miss Gurney among policemen still stands.

The end of 1953 and most of 1954 was dominated by the name of one man, Billy Graham. The churches were looking forward to the visit of the American evangelist who had been drawing large crowds and was now planning a Greater London crusade at Harringay Stadium in north London. Was it merely coincidence that the test explosion of a hydrogen bomb in the Pacific on 1 March took place on the very day that the crusade opened at Harringay? A conjunction of events that was altogether undesigned on the human level may, nevertheless, have been intended by God in his providence to impress the consciences of men. Whatever scoffers may have said or thought about it, many Christian people believed, with Dr Billy Graham himself, that there was a significance in the synchronisation of the two happenings which could not be idly dismissed as mere chance. Many police officers came to faith as a result of that crusade, and some of their testimonies appeared in the *OOD* magazine.

God had used many good Christian women to reach out to the police, and naturally enough we have focused on those who were in some way linked with the ICPA, founded by Catherine Gurney. But in 1875, eight years before the ICPA was officially established, Miss Mary Fry began meetings for both the Royal Irish Constabulary and the Dublin Metropolitan Police. These were held in Merrion Hall, Dublin, every Sunday afternoon and were still going in 1955. Sadly, Mary Fry passed away on the 10 August that year at the great age of ninety-eight and was sorely missed. But she would have been proud of a meeting that took place the following year on Sunday 29 April.

In the heart of HQ camp of the Irish Army at the Curragh Camp, County Kildare, about 300 people met together for the *Garda Siochána* police meeting. Sergeant Groves from Crumlin Station in Dublin presided over the meeting. Gordon Bourke from Raheny Station, County Dublin and *Garda* Gardiner from Kilmainham Station in Dublin city also took part. The big surprise for all present was the final speaker of the day, Bob Sproule. Bob, formerly a member of a notorious group known as The Nolan and Lavery Gang, had previously broken out of Mountjoy Prison before being recaptured and sent to Maryborough Convict Prison. It was after his release from there that he had a remarkable conversion experience and had become an itinerant preacher with a wonderful true story to tell.

Meanwhile, back in the south of England, the ICPA had taken a step of faith and appointed Miss Marjorie Upcher as honorary travelling representative. Over a six-month period, she worked her way through ten counties visiting over forty police establishments, having personal interviews with twelve chief constables who showed a real practical interest in the work of the ICPA. At that time, there were still a number of city and borough Police Forces as well as the County Constabularies.

With the support of the chief constables, Miss Upcher was able to leave copies of the ICPA magazine and other literature in police training centres. They had also made it possible for her to speak to groups of officers from fifteen to sixty strong, as well as to recruits. Such was the positive effect of her ministry that it was hoped that before long a colleague would be found to exercise a similar work in the north.

It should be remembered that the Association still had the word 'International' in its title and reports from overseas groups were welcomed. Former constable Alf Martin, who had emigrated to New Zealand, had been active in setting up an ICPA group in Auckland. Monthly meetings were being held with a core group of ten Christian officers. Meanwhile, also in the southern hemisphere, there was the ICPA's counterpart, the Christian Police and Prison Services Association. They had a large voluntary membership of 7,500 drawn from the South African police, prison officers and South African Railway and Harbours police. The head office was in Pretoria from where they distributed a monthly magazine in both Afrikaans and English under the title '*Ons Dien*' – 'We Serve'.

At home, the Police Missionary Union was still very active and was sending out New Testaments in English, French and Portuguese to police officers in Southern Rhodesia, Ghana, France and Brazil.

During that period, one of the biggest challenges to Western Christians was the phenomenal rise of the Korean Church. An elder from an American church had met a Korean pastor and asked him, 'How many do you get out to your prayer meetings?' 'About eighty,' replied the pastor. 'Why, you are no further along than we are,' said the visitor. 'We get that many out ourselves back in California on Wednesday evenings.' 'Oh,' said the surprised Korean, 'if you are talking of the Wednesday night service, we get 800 out for that. I thought you meant our daily dawn prayer meetings. About eighty of our people come at five o'clock every morning to pray.'

With growth in the Eastern Church progressing, there was still much work to be done in the UK. It was a time of building up and restoration – it was still only thirteen years since the devastation of the Second World War. A study of the nation's infrastructure had concluded that the future lay in road travel and so an ambitious project of road building had been undertaken. Before the end of the decade, sections of both the M1 and M6 motorways had been opened.

Motorways would not have been a lot of help to an Israeli police officer in Haifa who was trying to capture a team of smugglers. They used an ass-drawn caravan to escape. The policeman managed to capture some of the asses, though the smugglers got away. The clever officer let the beasts of burden go without food and then he turned them loose. Just as the officer had expected (knowing that in Isaiah 1:3 it says 'The ox knoweth his owner, and the ass his master's crib', KJV), the starving animals led the police directly to the smugglers' hideout!

The end of the decade would see some far-reaching changes for the ICPA. At the end of 1958, John Willamson was appointed president of the Association, and Sir Charles Martin, CBE, who had previously been Chief Constable of Liverpool, but was now one of Her Majesty's Inspectors of Constabulary, became chairman of the ICPA Council. A special meeting of the Council agreed that in future, the International Christian Police Association should be known as the Christian Police Association. It was felt that this was a more accurate and appropriate title. It was also decided at the same time that the designation director should be changed to secretary.

The change in leadership had come about due to the sudden death of Montague Goodman, the former president of the Association who, while attending a weekend conference at Hildenborough Hall, had fallen and broken his leg. Although taken to hospital and operated on, he sadly died on 31 October 1958 during his eighty-fourth year.

It was only six months later that the chairman and president swapped roles as news broke that would rock the Association. After twenty-three years' loyal service, George Paisley announced his retirement from the CPA. Writing the editorial of the magazine for the last time, he said,

> I have had a happy 23 years in this work. It has not been without its failures and disappointments, its heartaches and pains. You cannot nurture and bring up children without sleepless nights! Nevertheless I look back over the years with thankfulness to God "who hath enabled me, for that he counted me faithful, putting me into this ministry". The time has now come for me to hand over the work to another and younger man, and I know that the confidence you have placed in me will be bestowed upon the man who will follow in my steps.

Regrettably, due to ill health, he was unable to complete his last two months in post. The Council, as a temporary measure, decided to appoint Dorothy Kenning as acting secretary until a new general secretary could be appointed. Miss Kenning was well known to many officers as she had served as Lady Superintendent of the Police Convalescent Home at Hove from 1938 to 1954.

In a tribute to George Paisley, John Williamson wrote,

> It was a great blow to every member of the Christian Police Association when it was made known that our devoted and beloved Secretary had intimated to the Council that he wished to retire from the leadership of the Association on July 31st 1959. During his 23 years in office as Secretary, Mr Paisley won the confidence and goodwill of members and friends and had the satisfaction of seeing the Association lifted up to a high spiritual level not exceeded since the days of the Founder, Miss Catherine Gurney. Probably the greatest work Mr Paisley did was to edit the magazine *On and Off Duty* and to maintain its flow to all parts of the world.

Although the name had changed, the CPA still maintained its international links and the final edition of *OOD* for 1959 reprinted an article by former captain Conrad Jensen of the New York Police Department entitled, 'What is a Cop?'

> Cops are human (believe it or not) just like the rest of us. They come in both sexes but mostly male. They also come in various sizes. This sometimes depends on whether you are looking for one or trying to hide something. However, they are mostly big.
>
> Cops are found everywhere – on land, on the sea, in the air, on horses, in cars, and sometimes in your hair. In spite of the fact that 'you can't find one when you want one', they are usually there when it counts most. The best way to get one is to pick up the phone.
>
> Cops deliver lectures, babies and bad news. They are required to have the wisdom of Solomon, the disposition

of a lamb and muscles of steel and are often accused of having a heart to match. He's the one who rings the doorbell, swallows hard and announces the passing of a loved one; then spends the rest of the day wondering why he ever took such a crummy job.

On TV a cop is an oaf who couldn't find a bull fiddle in a telephone booth. In real life he is expected to find a little blond boy 'about so high' in a crowd of half a million people. In fiction he gets help from private eyes, reporters and 'who-dun-it' fans. In real life, mostly all he gets from the public is 'I didn't see nuttin'.'

When he serves a summons he's a monster. If he lets you go, he's a doll. To little kids he's either a friend or a bogeyman, depending on how the parents feel about it. He works 'around the clock', split shifts, Sundays and holidays and it always kills him when a joker says, 'hey, tomorrow is election day, I'm off, let's go fishing' (that's the day he works 20 hours).

A cop is like the little girl, who, when she was good, was very, very good, but when she was bad she was horrid. When a cop is good 'he's getting paid for it'. When he makes a mistake, he's a [disgrace] and that goes for the rest of them too. When he shoots a stick-up man he's a hero, except when the stick-up man is 'only a kid, anybody could'a seen that'.

Lots of them have homes, some of them covered with ivy, but most of them covered with mortgages. If he drives a big car, he's a [scammer]; a little car 'who's he kidding?' His credit is good; this is very helpful, because his salary isn't. Cops raise lots of kids; most of them belong to other people.

A cop sees more misery, bloodshed, trouble and sunrises than the average person. Like the postman, cops must also be out in all kinds of weather. His uniform changes with the climate, but his outlook on life remains about the same; mostly blank, but hoping for a better world.

Cops like days off, vacations and coffee. They don't like auto horns, family fights and anonymous letter writers. They have unions, but they can't strike. They must be impartial, courteous and always remember the slogan 'At Your Service'. This is sometimes hard especially when a character reminds him, 'I'm a tax payer, I pay your salary'.

Cops get medals for saving lives, stopping runaway horses and shooting it out with bandits (once in a while his widow gets the medal). But sometimes the most rewarding moment comes with some small kindness to an older person, he feels the warm hand clasp, looks into grateful eyes and hears 'Thank you and God bless you, son.'

The danger faced by police officers was also highlighted in an article about the brave actions of two London policewomen.

A task which no policewoman likes is to act as decoy in trapping a sex criminal. Yet when the job has to be done, she is always ready. Woman police constable Kathleen Parrot was attacked and badly hurt in East Croydon on her way home one night. After five weeks' sick leave she went coolly back to the tree-lined footpath where she had been injured. A male colleague hid nearby. From the trees a man leapt at the girl, brandishing a cosh. Policemen rushed him from cover, but he got away.

Later that night Sergeant Ethel Bush took over as decoy. With terrifying speed, the criminal struck again. By the time help reached the woman sergeant, she lay unconscious. Her attacker was arrested, tried and sentenced to ten years in jail. Seven months later both women were awarded the George Medal.

Although such bravery made headlines, there was another side of policing which also caught the attention of the press – corruption. Following two high-profile scandals involving borough Police Forces in Brighton and Nottingham, the Government set up a Royal Commission on the Police in 1960. Chaired by Sir Henry Willink, the brief of the commission would be wide-ranging and include:

- the constitution and functions of police authorities
- the accountability of police officers including chief constables
- the relationship of the police to the public and procedures for dealing with complaints
- the remuneration of police constables.

Rev Peter James

It would be a further two years before the final report was published, and the effects would include a large number of Force amalgamations and a large increase in pay for all police officers. If changes were afoot for the Police Service at the start of this decade, they were also coming to the CPA. Following the retirement of George Paisley in 1959, the Council advertised for a successor and in early 1960 appointed the Rev Peter James as the new general secretary. Before entering Christian ministry, Peter had been a teacher in Surrey, but following ordination into the Church of England, held various pastorates around England and Wales. At the time of his appointment, he was rector of Saint John the Evangelist Church, Little Leighs in Essex, and would divide his time between parish duties and the CPA.

On another front, this would be a new departure for the CPA and, for the first time in its history, the Association's headquarters moved away from London. Up until that time, the CPA and London had been synonymous, but with the move to Essex came the need to reorganise the function of the Association in the London area. It was decided that a London Branch should be formed with its own organising committee and that they would meet regularly on the fourth Thursday of each month.

With all these changes happening, it was perhaps no surprise that Miss Marjorie Upcher, who had been the honorary travelling representative since 1956, decided it was time to lay down her work, having moved to Cheltenham in 1958. But the next twelve months would bring even more changes.

The Council of the CPA, which until that time had met monthly in London, now decided that in future it would meet only once a year. In the intervening periods an Executive Committee nominated by the Council from among its own members would carry on the work. They felt that this would make for greater efficiency and also for a wider representation on the Council, who would ultimately be responsible for all matters of policy.

It was while looking at membership of the CPA that the Council had made another momentous decision. They were anxious to enlist the support of Christians outside the Police Service who shared their concern for the spiritual welfare of their colleagues in the police. The solution was to introduce associate membership for Christians who were not police officers but wanted to identify with the CPA and signified their agreement with the aims and basis of faith of the Association. This category of membership would also enable civilian staff in the police to come into fellowship with the Association.

Linking with Christians outside the Police Service received another boost when, in 1961, the Gideons International (an organisation founded in the USA to distribute Bibles and Testaments) commenced work printing 'Police' New Testaments. These were standard, pocket-sized copies of the New Testament and Psalms, but to differentiate them from Testaments given to individuals and other organisations, they were bound in a blue cover. Many opportunities ensued to both present and place the Testaments in police training establishments.

Identification with the police was an important issue for the CPA, and the Council began examining the badge of the Association. The existing one had served well for the previous ten years, but after much thought, consultation and prayer, it was decided that a change was desirable. Three factors had to be borne in mind when designing the new badge. Firstly, it needed to be identified quietly with membership of the Police Service, and so a small symbolic police helmet was incorporated. Secondly, being an association based on the principles of the Word of God, an open Bible was included. Thirdly, having a desire to be known as those who were positively Christian, the foregoing symbols would be placed on a shield, representing faith with a centrally placed cross to present Christ as the answer to the deepest needs of humankind. Along with these would be the new initials of the Association 'CPA'. And so in 1962 the new badge became available.

It is sometimes in the oddest of places that little gems are found, and in the March/April edition of *OOD* a prayer for motorists was suggested, which apparently been seen in a road safety communication:

> Help me, O God, as I drive, to love my neighbour as myself, that I may do nothing to hurt or endanger any of your children. Give to my eyes clear vision, and skill to my hands and feet. Make me tranquil in mind and relaxed

in body. Deliver from the spirit of rivalry and from all resentment at the actions of others, and bring me safe to my journey's end. Grant this, O Father, for the sake of Him who loved us and gave His life for us, Jesus Christ our Lord. Amen.

One person who had safely come to her journey's end was Miss Aphra White at the splendid age of ninety-one. She was one of the grand 'old warriors' of the CPA whose particular interest was in the Police Missionary Union. The Union had once been a flourishing part of the Association, collecting funds to send Bibles and Testaments to police officers in other countries. In recent years, however, the work had shrunk to just one branch, based in Lavender Hill, south London; ironically the very area where Catherine Gurney had been born! Following Aphra White's death, the work of the Union was absorbed into the CPA headquarters.

Shortly after this, a report was received from Nigeria where police officers on duty at a police college had stopped a car belonging to the Niger-Challenge Press of the Sudan Interior Mission and asked for copies of the New Testament, which were willingly given to them. Their duties had prevented them being present when over 300 policemen and women made an impressive sight as they marched to their Assembly Hall to receive New Testaments as a gift from the Scripture Gift Mission, presented by the Rev Harold Fuller, editor of the African *Challenge*.

The early 1960s seemed to be a period when many stalwarts were lost to the Association. One such person was Horace Elphick, who had joined the Metropolitan Police in 1901. Former chief constable, John Williamson, CBE said of him, 'He was affectionately known to his large number of friends in the CPA as Uncle Horace. He was a Christian warrior with an amazing touch. He was quiet, thorough, reliable, active,

Horace Elphick

discerning, patient, never in a hurry to go before, or lag behind.' Horace was very active in his faith and in the CPA. He retired from the police as an inspector in 1927, but still remained active in the Association. He passed to his rest on 4 April 1962.

One of the most noticeable changes in the lifetime of Horace Elphick was the decline in membership of the CPA. The Great War and Second World War had taken their toll on young Christian men, and the scale of violence and misery had caused many to lose or question their faith. Added to this was the fact that many CPA groups around the country had been organised and run by Christians outside the Police Service who had either known or been influenced by Catherine Gurney. These too had gradually passed away, leaving a leadership vacuum that sometimes was unable to be filled.

When counting up the membership numbers in 1962, it was found that there were only 455 who were in touch with the CPA headquarters. However, a problem discovered and never really resolved was that many others in the police received the *OOD* magazine and were in touch with local branches but had never committed themselves to membership. They were often most surprised to find that they were not members, as they had considered themselves part of the Association.

Perhaps part of the problem was the perception of what the CPA was all about. Early in 1963 Peter James highlighted the aims of the Association at that time which were

- to draw together the members of the Christian Police Association in a bond of Christian love, fellowship and prayer
- to witness before members of the Police Service a high ideal of life made possible through faith in the Lord Jesus Christ
- to enlist the support and fellowship of those, both at home and overseas, who sought the spiritual welfare of members of the Police Service.

He said, 'There are those who think that the Association exists primarily for the provision of teams and speakers.' Another view of the CPA was expressed by a member some time later who said that some people thought it was about 'ties, teas and cucumber sandwiches'. Quite an indictment on how the CPA was projecting its message!

With change in the air, it was announced in May that year that John Williamson had resigned as Chairman of Council, having held that position for eighteen years. He had been the first police officer to serve on the Council when appointed in 1932. His place as chairman would be taken by Stanley Harrison, a sergeant in the Metropolitan Police, who was soon to retire. In addition, Sir Charles Martin, one of Her Majesty's Inspectors of Constabulary, former Chief Constable of Liverpool City Police, who had been president since 1959, felt that due to pressure of work and subsequent lack of time he should resign.

Perception of the Association was one thing, but always high on the agenda for CPA members was personal behaviour as emphasised in the aims mentioned above. Police officers all over the world were well aware of the results of bad behaviour often commencing at a very early age. This led to some officers in the Houston, Texas, Police

Department to pen a tongue-in-cheek article, 'Twelve Rules for Delinquency':

1. Begin with infancy to give the child everything he wants. This way, he will grow up to believe the world owes him a living.
2. When he picks up bad words, laugh at him. This will make him think he's cute. It will also encourage him to pick up cuter phrases that will blow the top off your head later.
3. Never give him spiritual training. Wait until he is 21 and then let him decide for himself.
4. Avoid using the word 'wrong'. It may develop a guilt complex. Besides, it will condition him to believe later, when he is arrested for stealing a car, that society is against him and he is being persecuted.
5. Pick up everything he leaves lying around – toys, books, shoes, clothes. Do everything for him so that he will be experienced in throwing all responsibility on others.
6. Let him read any printed matter he can get his hands on. Be careful that the silverware and drinking glasses are sterilised, but let his mind feast on garbage.
7. Quarrel frequently in the presence of your children. In this way they will not be too shocked when the home is broken up later.
8. Give a child all the spending money he wants. Never let him earn his own. Why should he have things as tough as you had them?
9. Satisfy his cravings for food, drink and comfort. See that his sensual desire is gratified. Denial may lead to harmful frustration.
10. Take his part against neighbours, teachers, authorities. They are all prejudiced against your child.
11. When he gets into real trouble, apologise for yourself by saying 'I never could do anything with him.'
12. Prepare for a life of grief. You will be likely to have it.

Around this time a number of Police Forces had taken up the idea of training young people. Young men and some young women were encouraged to become police cadets and larger Forces had dedicated training centres for them. At one such centre near Ashford in Kent, an inspector, who himself had recently become a member of the CPA, was encouraging cadets who passed through to find fellowship through meeting together. Just outside the centre was a bungalow owned by a dear old Christian lady known as 'Granny Wilson', and regular meetings were held there. She liked to refer to the cadets as 'her boys' and, although riddled with arthritis, would use the night hours to pray for those in the training centre.

With a renewed impetus in the work of the CPA and only having a part-time general secretary, further help was needed to run the Association. George Gladdish, who had been a detective chief inspector in the Fingerprint Branch at New Scotland Yard, and who retired in 1963, took up the part-time post of administrative secretary, with his wife, Vera, assisting as office secretary. It was not just the management of members in the UK that had to be taken care of as the CPA still accepted members from overseas.

It was always good to learn of the enthusiasm and dedication of Christians in the Police Service, but the CPA was now coming to know more of other Christians when they joined as associate members. One such was Fred Lemon, a habitual burglar who had come to faith while serving a sentence in HM Prison Dartmoor. His changed life was evident, and during a Devon Branch weekend in 1965 he had shared his exciting story, commenting that he never thought

Fred Lemon

125

that he would willingly stand on the same platform as police officers. Fred decided to cement that link with Christian police officers by becoming an associate member in 1966.

In another move which raised the profile of the Association that year, the Billy Graham Evangelistic Association invited the CPA to provide stewards with special responsibilities at the Greater London Crusade at Earls Court, every night from 1 June to 2 July, in both a practical and advisory capacity under the leadership of Station Sergeant Robin Oake, an instructor in the Metropolitan Police Training School. This included, on one occasion, ensuring the safety of Billy Graham when he decided to go and preach in the open air in London's Soho district.

In May that year, Home Secretary Roy Jenkins took powers under the Police Act 1964 to announce that the number of Police Forces in England and Wales was to be reduced from 117 to forty-nine, and where local authorities did not agree voluntarily, he would make the amalgamations compulsory. While being done on the grounds of efficiency, it would mean that many officers would have to swallow their pride of force and adapt to new ways of working.

But perhaps the biggest event to shock the Police Service and the nation occurred on 12 August 1966 near HM Prison Wormwood Scrubs in west London. Not since the Houndsditch Murders in 1910 had there been such outrage. Three plainclothes police officers in an unmarked police vehicle spotted three men in a battered estate car parked near the prison. Two of the officers got out to question the occupants, whereupon the front passenger produced a handgun and shot one of the officers, killing him instantly. The other officer ran back to the police car but was pursued and also shot. The rear passenger got out and, approaching the police car, shot the driver three times. That incident is still known today as the Shepherd's Bush Murders.

As a result of this incident, the Police Dependants' Trust was established to assist the families of police officers in Britain who had been killed or injured on duty. This was a much-needed and welcome addition to the welfare of such officers provided by the convalescent homes in the north and south of the country, and the work of the Gurney Fund and St George's Fund in supporting the children of police officers who had died in service.

The Police Seaside Home at Hove (formerly West Brighton) in Sussex had been enlarged several times since its official opening in 1893 and, due to increasing demand, it was now time to take the next step. Just a month after the shootings at Shepherd's Bush, the convalescent home moved to a new building at 205 Kingsway, Hove, right on the seafront. It was officially opened in November 1966 by Her Majesty Queen Elizabeth, the Queen Mother.

There was still a need to raise the profile of the CPA and gain the support of the Christian public. One opportunity was the Christian Holiday Crusade held at Filey in Yorkshire where more than 5,000 people would gather annually to hear a variety of speakers and learn of missionary groups, at home and overseas, in the exhibitions. Since 1964 the organisers, the Movement for World Evangelisation, had requested the assistance of the CPA to assist on the campsite, for times when the youthful exuberance and high-spiritedness of a small minority threatened to spoil the holiday for others. Being given the opportunity to have a small display stand in the Home Missions exhibition proved valuable and many useful contacts were made.

Due to the previously mentioned Force amalgamations,

no new branches were formed during 1967, but there was still an increase in membership, with 129 new applications during the year.

It is said that you 'can't keep a good man down', and within CPA circles there have been many who have felt God's call to serve him in leadership roles. One name that has surfaced time and time again is that of John Williamson. Having stood down as chairman of the Association in 1963, he continued to serve as a member of Council, but it was with great pleasure that it was announced in 1968 that he had accepted an invitation to be reappointed as president of the Association.

As the Police Service was going through great changes in organisation and structure, it was an opportune time for the CPA to examine itself. A conference was held at Hothorpe Hall in Leicestershire, where it was unanimously agreed to revise the aims of the Association as follows:

- to promote and foster the fellowship of Christian police officers in that unity which is enjoyed by those who are born again by the Spirit of God
- to demonstrate this relationship to God in a concern for righteousness both on and off duty
- and to obey Christ in proclaiming his gospel, especially to members of the Police Service that they might be brought to know him personally.

Following the conference it was also announced that Stan Harrison had resigned as Chairman of Council for personal reasons. In his place, Inspector Robin Oake (London) had been appointed with Gordon A'Court (East Glamorgan) as vice-chairman. With all the amalgamations that had taken place, it was less than a year before the East Glamorgan Branch had requested a name-change to 'South Wales Branch'.

Robin Oake

The end of the decade saw much civil unrest in Northern Ireland, with rioting in Belfast and Londonderry. The Royal Ulster Constabulary were overwhelmed and had received a lot of criticism. Finally, the British Government sent in British Army troops, with the first detachment arriving on 15 August 1969. With a strong branch of the CPA in Northern Ireland it was right that their voice should be heard, and an extract from their branch magazine was included in *OOD* that November.

> It is very difficult to write about the tragic happenings in our province in these days but it would be wrong to pass over them in silence. They have been denounced and deplored by leaders of the church and state and certainly will win no sympathy from right thinking people. Surely the situation calls for humiliation and prayer on the part of us all. It may well be our witness has often lacked faithfulness and spiritual power. If so, let us acknowledge this and seek renewal and forgiveness from God. We, as members of the CPA, must deplore the unjust criticism of our Force in recent days; our men have faced up to difficult and dangerous situations, always conscious of their duty as officers of the law, a duty which they sought to do impartially. We also need to pray for all our leaders that in these critical days they may know the enabling of God, in seeking to make possible a return to sanity, so that we may live quiet and peaceful lives in all godliness.

Suspicion is the stock-in-trade of police officers. A combination of obvious facts combined with a gut feeling that something is wrong has helped many an officer to 'feel a collar'. But sometimes that same suspicion turns inward and police officers look for real or perceived threats from within. At the beginning of the 1970s, allegations started to appear in print concerning the influence of Freemasonry in the Police Service. It was said that officers' careers had been made or broken because they were, or were not, Freemasons. It was alleged that the oath taken by Freemasons was not a harmless charade, but that it seriously conflicted with the oath of allegiance to the Sovereign which all officers took upon attestation.

While these allegations were denied, it was not long before counter-allegations were made and it was suggested that the CPA was some sort of secret society. Because officers of different ranks met together at CPA gatherings, the inference was that some sort of preferment was being offered to members. Of course, such allegations were without foundation, as senior officers who were members of the Association had always been careful to show scrupulous fairness when it came to promotions.

Difficult issues have to be faced, and it was during this period that Peter James was having his own personal struggle with ministry in the Church of England. Feeling that it was no longer tenable for him, he resigned from his parish and moved from the rectory to 9 Park Street, Thaxted, Dunmow in Essex, taking the headquarters of the CPA with him. At the same time, George Gladdish felt it was time to relinquish his post, having served since 1964. Before the end of 1970 there were to be more changes as Peter accepted a call to become the minister of Bristol Road Baptist Church in Weston-super-Mare and on his move, resigned from his position in the CPA.

Chapter 7

Taking a stand for one's faith has always been important to CPA members, whether on or off duty, and this was evidenced by the actions of traffic patrol officer PC Graham Bailey, who had been offered a number of machines to race in the Isle of Man Production Machine TT Classic. He made it clear that he would not take part on Sundays because of his Christian beliefs, but would compete only in a Saturday international. Echoes here of Scotsman Eric Liddell's stand at the 1924 Olympics when he refused to race on a Sunday.

Another man noted for his faith was Ivor Fox. He was the first and only secretary of the Cornwall Branch before the Force was amalgamated with Devon. Ivor would tell anyone who would listen that the most memorable date in his life had been in 1956 when, with his wife, Margaret, he had solemnly made a stand of faith and taken Jesus Christ to be his Saviour. In a tribute paid at his funeral in August 1970 it was said of him that 'he was a great man, and a first-class copper too!' What better epithet could someone have?

In March that year, with the resignation of George Gladdish, the Council had appointed the Rev George Roberts to succeed him as administrative secretary. However, when the Rev Peter James departed the CPA, George Roberts was requested by the Council to take over as general secretary.

George had been inducted into the pastorate of Thaxted Baptist Church in September 1970 and took up residence in the manse next door with his wife, Anna, and three young children. Originally from Northern Ireland, he had trained at the Faith Mission Bible College and worked as an evangelist with them before going to work with the YMCA in Ireland. In 1957, he

Rev George Roberts

moved to Deptford in south-east London where he became pastor of the Princess Louise Institute. Before being called to the work of the CPA, George had founded and directed the Christian Counsel Telephone Service.

As he took up the reins of the CPA, so it was reported that another stalwart had gone to her rest. Marjorie Upcher, honorary travelling secretary of the Association, had died on 23 November at the age of eighty-eight years.

In the midst of all the staff changes, one could be forgiven for thinking that the normal work of the CPA was somehow neglected, but this was not the case. Officers were still proclaiming their faith in word and deed and across the UK. CPA witness teams were taking church services almost every weekend. Using friends and family to make contact with police officers had always been part of the Association's ethos, and so it perhaps came as no surprise to learn that Betty A'Court, sister of the South Wales Branch secretary Gordon A'Court, had made contact with a number of officers in Belgium where she was working with the Belgian Gospel Mission.

Building on these contacts led to the first visit of a CPA witness team outside of Great Britain. In November 1970, a team consisting of Inspector Robin Oake (Metropolitan), Sergeant Gordon A'Court (South Wales), Constable Wesley McKenzie (Royal Ulster Constabulary) and Detective Constable Margaret Guillebaud (Metropolitan) travelled to Belgium where they took services in local churches and met with a number of Belgian police officers. This was the first of many such visits and led to the formation of a CPA Extension into Europe Sub-Committee to oversee these and other teams going to Europe.

Back in the UK, George Roberts had been very well accepted and had been making regular visits to branches. He had been assisted since May 1971 by the Rev Graham Pickhaver, minister of Sible Hedingham Baptist Church, in running the Association. However, Robin Oake expressed his concerns at the end of 1971 concerning the post of general secretary being only part-time. While there was much encouragement, the accumulating administrative work and the pastoral demands within the Association placed a heavy burden on George Roberts.

No doubt, though, it would have gladdened George's heart when he received the report of the 1971 Annual Gospel Campaign in Portrush, Northern Ireland, organised by the local CPA branch. In spite of the violence and threats in the Province, many officers were able to gather for the week-long event and hear ministry from the well-known Ulster preacher Willie Mullan, from Lurgan. Although there were some doubts about holding open-air services, the branch were tremendously encouraged when nearly 1,500 people attended these daily gatherings to proclaim the good news of God's salvation.

If one word could sum up the work of the CPA during 1971 it would be 'renewal'. There was renewed fellowship, renewed vision and in some measure, renewed outreach to colleagues. With Graham Pickhaver on board as assistant general secretary, the Association had been able to get back to producing its magazine bi-monthly. Commenting on this, George Roberts noted that 'to be effective the magazine should provide three things: information, instruction and inspiration. We need information to direct us in our prayers for each other. We need instruction to assist our spiritual growth and we need inspiration to drive us forward.' He also notes that he had recently heard of a number of people who had covenanted to pray at a specific time each day for the CPA.

Often *OOD* had reprinted words of wisdom from senior officers who also held Christian faith, and in the April 1972 edition it carried the following remarks from the Assistant Chief Constable of Leicester and Rutland Constabulary, Mr C James Anderton:

> In my view it is more important today than ever in the past for those who find themselves in authority over others, or in any position of influence of leadership in the community, to show not only the necessary professional knowledge and skills, but also the highest possible standards of personal behaviour and moral integrity. All police officers, whatever their rank, are leaders in the community, and have a special part to play in strengthening and maintaining Christian virtues for the common good. In the Police Force, as in all public services, the personal example of the members is vital. We should all strive to ensure that we live and do our duty by righteous principles.

April 1972 was to be another significant milestone for the Association. Chief Constable David McNee, City of Glasgow Police, and a CPA vice-president, officially launched the John Williamson Fund at the Annual Meetings. Two months earlier, when the Council had met together in Glasgow, after a morning of prayer and praise, they took the decision to appoint a full-time general secretary and purchase a permanent headquarters for the work. The purpose of the fund was three-fold – firstly, to finance a full-time general secretary; secondly, to purchase a headquarters in Leicester; and thirdly, for the ongoing work of the Association. In launching the fund, David McNee said, 'John Williamson has been the man behind the Association for as long as I can remember ... He is not concerned with the wellbeing of himself here today but with the "well done" of the Master.'

With a massive response to the appeal, matters progressed rapidly, and after some weeks of anticipation and preparation, the CPA moved into its new headquarters on 31 July 1972. Named 'John Williamson House' in honour of the man who had done so much for the Association, it was situated at 5 Mosse Way, Oadby, Leicester, that area having been chosen as its geographic location made it relatively easy to get to from most

John Williamson House

parts of the country. A Thanksgiving Service and Dedication of John Williamson House took place on 23 September 1972 when the speakers were Inspector Robin Oake and John Williamson Esq, CBE, KPM.

The relocation of the headquarters meant a reorganisation of staff. An office extension was to be built onto the house at Oadby and upon its completion at the end of April 1973, the Rev Graham Pickhaver would relinquish his responsibilities as assistant general secretary. In the meantime, Mrs Mavis Harrold joined the staff at the beginning of December 1972 and would ultimately assume responsibility for the day-to-day management of the office.

Meanwhile, CPA members and associates were getting on with their normal duties and using their gifts wherever they could. One talented associate member was Chris Porteous, a solicitor with the Metropolitan Police. Musing one day on what a police officer might have made of the incarnation of Jesus Christ, he wrote a poem entitled 'The Christmas Arrest'.[9]

It was early Christmas morning. I was walking on my beat
When I stopped this man and woman who were loitering in the street.
They had a little baby boy wrapped up in swathing bands
Asleep inside a carry cot they carried in their hands.

I stopped them on suspicion that the girl was on the game.
She called him 'Joseph Carpenter' and 'Mary' was her name.
They did not seem to have a home or other fixed abode,
I took them to the station which was just across the road.

I searched his trouser pockets as required by the law.
I only found a census form and little bits of straw.
I left the woman constable to make a search of her,
And in the baby's carry cot was frankincense and myrrh.

They said the baby boy was theirs, but called him 'Son of God',
And said they had to hide him here away from one, Herod;
We checked them in the phone book and we searched at CRO,
We fed them in the staff canteen and then we let them go.

I made an entry in my book and went to find the car,
When right above the station yard there shone an eastern star;
Angels on the telephone were ringing up the station,
And written on the message pad was 'Jesus, our salvation'.

The poem was set to music and sung at the very first Metropolitan Police Carol Service at All Souls Church, Langham Place, in December 1974. Prior to being sung, it was recited by actor Jack Warner who, as previously mentioned, had played the role of PC George Dixon in the film *The Blue Lamp* and in the television series *Dixon of Dock Green*.

Humour is often used in the Police Service as individuals try to come to terms with some of the more difficult tasks they face on a regular basis. Officers are also known for having a laugh even when it is at their own expense. If 'The Christmas Arrest' was pure fiction, the following story related by PC Stanley Shepherd, then branch secretary for West Yorkshire, is certainly an 'arresting story'.

To be arrested is bad enough, but to be arrested for taking off a copper – when you are a copper – is a bit disconcerting to say the least. It turned out, however, to be the most humorous experience of my 16 years in the Bradford Force.

It came to pass in this way. It was the Annual Meeting at the Guildhall in London. Three of us decided to go. There was the village constable from Drighlington (who I will from now on call by his nickname 'flying vicar', so christened because of his reputation as a motorcyclist and Methodist local preacher), a Special from Bradford and yours truly. We could only get the one day off, so we decided to travel up to London overnight, and back the following night. We would use my grey Austin A35 van.

It was on the journey back that the excitement occurred. It had been a terrific day. Meeting old pals whom we hadn't seen for a year. Listening to reports from all over the country. And being sent on our way home rejoicing with an encouraging gospel message. We were on top of the world, but very, very tired. I took the wheel until we reached the A1, and then the flying vicar took over. My last words to him were, 'Don't forget that this is a commercial vehicle, and we are restricted to 40 miles per hour.' I must have been shattered, because I don't remember another thing until being awakened by a blue flashing light from a police car pulled up in front of us on the hard shoulder. 'He's been speeding!' I thought. But how wrong I was proved to be.

You see, a gang of thieves had been operating in the Leicestershire area, and were using a grey A35 van. And what is more to the point, they were pretending to be coppers in plain clothes. A few minutes previously, a wireless message had been sent out to all police cars in the vicinity of the A1 to the effect that the thieves were believed to be travelling north through Rutland. A patrol car was parked alongside the road, the driver and observer having a quiet burn. They were nevertheless keeping a sharp lookout at passing vehicles, and the second car to pass them after the message was a grey A35 van. Us! Sparks from the fag ends shot out of the patrol car windows as it screeched into pursuit. As we were pulled in, out jumped the two observant officers. The flying vicar wound the window down, and with a sickly smile on his face said, 'It's all right chum, we're police officers!' That just about disposed any doubts in the minds of the boys in blue that we were their men. I never knew exactly what happened. We were somehow hauled out of the van and made to stand with our hands above our heads. We were then frisked like a bunch of Chicago Hoods. We protested our innocence, but our words fell on stony ground. That was until checks were made with the West Yorkshire and Bradford Police headquarters. Then there was much back slapping and hand shaking, and 'No hard feelings?' And we were allowed to wend our weary way home.

But the force artist had been at the receiving end when the message of enquiry about our validity came in. A cartoon was consequently pinned to the notice board and this was perceived by the Public Relations Office. I was called in to give an explanation at the daily press conference and a few days later a column in one of the Nationals read 'Shadrach, Meshach and Abednego – Arrested on the A1 impersonating policemen!'

With CPA members being transformed into biblical characters, there were other transformations afoot. The start of 1974 saw a new editorial team for *OOD* headed by the former assistant general secretary, Graham Pickhaver. With different coloured backgrounds on each issue, it was hoped to present a modern image to a timeless message.

CPA president, John Williamson, had been commissioned by the editorial team to write a series of articles answering questions that were raised about being a Christian in the Police Service. The first of these dealt with the perceived conflict between allegiance to Christ and the demands of the Job and was published in the January edition. It was a shock, therefore, when it was announced that he had died on the morning of 4 April 1974 at the age of eighty-five.

Many paid tribute to him, but suffice to mention three who committed their reflections to print. Council chairman, Robin Oake, said of him,

> My principal recollections of 'The Chief' – as he was so affectionately known by many – are of his wisdom in conversation based so broadly on scriptures and on his vast Christian experience ... I came to recognise his rightful authority and alertness; his helpfulness and grace ... His anecdotes in meetings are treasured memories such as, 'I began by fearing the sergeant and God but ended my service fearing God!' He fought a good fight and finished the race – he kept the faith.

Fred Murphy from Northern Ireland wrote,

> The 'Chief' was a big man in every sense of the word – physically, mentally, and above all, spiritually. He was one of those who had that rare combination of power and gentleness – a spiritual Rolls-Royce. God endowed him with great gifts and from the time of his conversion, just before he joined the Police Service, he used these gifts for his wonderful Saviour, the Lord Jesus ... Some of his success in the Police Service led to his decorations

at Buckingham Palace when he was honoured by the conferment of the King's Police Medal and the CBE. But this success was more than matched in his spiritual life, when by the enabling power of God it can be said of him, like Paul, 'I have fought a good fight, I have finished my course, I have kept the faith.'

George Roberts had only known John Williamson for four years, but said, 'When I received the news of the passing of our beloved "Uncle John" I tried to assess the lessons I had learned.' He went on to say how he had seen the serenity of the man, his steadfastness of purpose and his identity as a spiritual man. He said, 'To use a phrase he used sometimes in reference to others, he had both "unction and gumption"!'

As they had already been written, the series of articles by John Williamson continued to be published in the CPA magazine and were also subsequently published as a separate booklet. As an individual, he was irreplaceable and a hard act to follow, but the Council needed to appoint

David McNee

a new president. They found such a man and after prayer and discussion, unanimously appointed David McNee to the role. At that time, he was Chief Constable of the City of Glasgow Police but soon after became chief constable of the amalgamated Scottish Forces which became Strathclyde Police. His service and dedication to policing were rewarded when, in the New Year's Honours List, he was awarded the Queen's Police Medal.

The dedication of the ordinary officers on the streets was noticed but as vehicle-related crime was on the increase, they often felt hindered by the lack of available information. So it was a great boon to them when the Police National Computer went live in 1974 with an index of stolen vehicles that could be accessed twenty-four hours a day. It has since grown to include many other databases providing information on people, vehicles, crimes and property.

Having good information prior to attending an incident is extremely useful, but there are times when officers just don't know anything until they arrive at the scene. One such incident was that attended by Essex PC David Barlow. On patrol with two other officers they were called to a violent domestic situation. On arrival they found an immensely strong drunken man surrounded by relatives. It was obvious that this man had to be arrested and David prayed that he would be given strength to deal with the situation. He went to the man, took his arm, and was amazed to find that the man was immediately calm and submissive to him. He was then taken to the police station. David had prayed that he would be given the strength to deal with the man, but the Lord had not answered this prayer as David expected, but rather had taken the power away from the man. The wisdom of this was apparent after the event, because had David used force to detain this man, undoubtedly all his relatives would have joined in, creating a very dangerous situation.

Following a year of relative stability in the CPA, 1976 was to see more staff changes. At the end of 1975 Mavis Harrold gave up her job of running the office and this was taken on by Mrs Brenda Brady, former secretary to the principal of London Bible College. No sooner was she in post than the Council received the news that its chairman, Chief Inspector Robin Oake, had been advised on medical grounds to drastically reduce his outside commitments and release himself from a large number of committees on which he was serving with great distinction. He had steered the Council through a period fraught with problems, into a period of sustained development. He had been chairman for eight-and-a-half years. Elected by the Council to succeed Robin was Inspector Jim Green (Metropolitan).

On a positive note, in spite of security issues, the Northern Ireland Branch were able to hold their first gospel campaign in Portrush after an absence of five years. There were representatives present from both sides of the Irish Sea, and all who attended were greatly encouraged.

Not many people like to see adverse publicity on any front, but one incident was to mar the late summer of 1976. In the very area that had spawned the CPA, officers were policing the normally peaceful Notting Hill Carnival. Racial tensions were high over the use of 'Stop and Search' powers among young black men. The tension boiled over and, although the flashpoint was uncertain, there was soon full-blown rioting, with ill-equipped police officers coming under attack from a hail of missiles. More than 100 officers were taken to hospital and the incident led to the implementation of the Race Relations Act, 1976 which prohibited racial discrimination.

Policing in difficult situations is not the prerogative of any one part of the world. Rhodesia (now Zimbabwe) had a branch of the CPA at this time, led by branch secretary George Knowles. He sent a report to the Association's headquarters in the UK telling of their first conference, which was held in Bulawayo the previous September. He concluded his report,

> We as a branch of CPA have been greatly blessed and encouraged by this first conference in Rhodesia, and

look to God for further blessing and witness amongst our members. We would ask prayer for our weekly CPA meeting held every Thursday evening, numbers vary as our policemen are away from time to time doing their bit for our country.

Police officers are used to facing difficult questions, and early in 1977 London Branch secretary, Don Axcell, was approached by Thames Television to take part in a late-night epilogue series entitled *Crime Gentlemen Please*. Having obtained permission from both the police and the CPA, Don was interviewed for the programme by Leonard Pearcey. In the short interview, Don tried to answer in a positive way the following questions:

1. What sort of effect does police work have on a Christian?
2. When you walk through the door as a policeman, presumably, when do you become a Christian as well as a policeman in action?
3. If you suddenly say 'I am a Christian', do they regard a Christian PC as an oddity?
4. What about your colleagues, how do they regard you as a Christian police officer?
5. What are the elements that they don't think go together that you obviously feel do go together?
6. They say that the Police Force is a graveyard for a Christian, don't they? Is that true?
7. How much have you yourself found yourself to be in need of help? In other words, what effect has your police work had on your faith?

In answer to the last question, Don's reply was, 'On my own faith, it has certainly strengthened it. I was a Christian when I came into the police and since I have been in, it has strengthened it, seeing other people in need in every sort of situation and realising that just as I needed to have a personal commitment to Christ, so these people too, whatever their need, need Jesus Christ as well.'

In March 1977, CPA president, David McNee, was appointed Commissioner of the Metropolitan Police. While this was an obvious promotion for him in the light of his distinguished police career, some saw the appointment as controversial, as no previous Scottish senior police officer had ever been parachuted into this top job. Others saw it as a snub to the hierarchy of the Metropolitan Police, still recovering from the anti-corruption campaign of the retiring Commissioner, Sir Robert Mark.

There were still security issues in Northern Ireland, and members of the RUC still came under attack, but George Roberts was determined to visit the province, meeting members, some of whom had been injured, and also the widows of officers killed by the IRA. On one evening he met with a group from Lurgan for fellowship and ministry. The theme that emerged from the meeting was that of the sovereign care of our risen Saviour and anticipation of his glory. Inspector Harold Cobb chaired that meeting and the closing hymn he had chosen was 'Face to Face with Christ my Saviour'. They talked afterwards about those who were feeling the strain of battle. Harold had a fatherly heart and the ability to encourage. After the meeting, George was asked to go along to the police station for some fellowship with an officer who had to leave the meeting immediately after it concluded. He left the station sometime after midnight. The following morning at 8.40 Harold Cobb was deliberately, cold-bloodedly, cruelly murdered, having been shot by IRA terrorists at a checkpoint in the town centre.

George was not one for sitting back and taking things easy. He affirmed his calling to the work of the CPA and wanted to take the Association forward. At the end of 1977 he wrote an article for the magazine called 'Looking Ahead'. In it he highlighted four areas where he would like to see progress.

1. The fulfilling of God's promises
It is the ultimate in foolishness to either look ahead or go ahead in dependence upon our own resources. Ours is a spiritual work and calls for spiritual qualities. Root and branch it finds its expression in the supernatural activity of Almighty God.

2. Facing our Problems
1978 presents problems that must be recognised and when recognised must be tackled. If we don't we shall find that we are constantly looking over our shoulder to make up for yesterday's inadequacies. [He requests prayer for the need of staff, equipment, facilities for an expanding work and outreach material.] The economic factors common to the whole of our society have forced us to cut back in all these areas.

3. The fulfilment of our purpose
Constantly we remind ourselves of our aim. Constantly we ask ourselves what is the purpose of our existence and many of you can quote from memory our stated purpose. This has been an excellent year for fellowship gatherings, but we have been severely restricted in our literature outreach. [He says,] Can we make communication of our faith a priority in 1978?

4. Fellowship in participation
As we look ahead are you prepared to play your part? A famous evangelist once said in reply to a letter from a friend who had written 'that he was with him in spirit', 'My good friend, I don't conduct meetings for spirits.' We want to increase our mailing list, not reduce it. We want to

function as 'salt' (Matthew 5:13) not fossilise into a 'holy huddle.' We desire to bring to the Police Service qualities of efficiency, integrity, compassion and all that makes for the highest good of that service and the whole community.

As seemed to be the ongoing pattern for the work, there was both encouraging news and setbacks during 1978. The year had started well, with the news that CPA president David McNee had received a knighthood in the New Year's Honours List and that Mr James Anderton, Chief Constable of Greater Manchester, had accepted the invitation to become a vice-president. Following the opportunity the previous year for Don Axcell to appear in a TV epilogue, Northumberland and Durham Branch secretary, Harry Wardle, had been invited by Tyne Tees television to give the morning prologue during Holy Week.

CPA headquarters had received a report from Jamaica via the Fellowship of Christian Peace Officers in the USA, written by Inspector Raymond Neita of the Jamaica Police who said, 'On Wednesday 18 May 1977 at about 7pm, eight committed Christian policemen met together to form the St James Chapter of the Christian Police Association. This is an international body with headquarters in England. The St James Chapter is the first of its kind in Jamaica, and already plans have been made to establish various chapters throughout Jamaica.'

On the home front, there were issues to be faced. In the office, Brenda Brady had left and been replaced by Harold Wiles, a former principal officer with the Land Registry. Mrs Gea Champness had joined the staff to give secretarial help, thus easing the burden on George Roberts. *OOD* editor Graham Pickhaver and his team were having great difficulties and, in the short term, faced a losing battle against escalating costs. This had led to a reduction in the number of issues produced. Independent professional advice had suggested closure of the magazine at the end of 1978 to be replaced with a monthly newsletter to branch secretaries and Council members. However, after ninety-five years of continual production, the Council were most reluctant to act on this advice.

Finance had become a real issue, with a serious shortfall in income. Drastic cutbacks needed to be made and in addition to reducing production of the magazine, the general secretary's salary had been held at the 1975 level and his car, financed by the CPA, had not been replaced. Alan Harris, an assistant bank manager with Barclays Bank, who had been an associate member for fifteen years, had agreed to accept the role of treasurer for the Association.

With the strain of events, the mood of the Council was concerned but still upbeat. They accepted that many of the conditions prevailing at the time when Catherine Gurney founded the Association were still to be overcome in 1978. They believed that the CPA still had a message and manner of life that were relevant to the Police Service. It was a shock when, on 17 June, George Roberts was admitted to hospital with a heart attack. Thankfully, he recovered from that trauma and returned to work.

With threats of closure hanging over the magazine, the editorial team still found time to raise the spirits with a humorous tale. Titled 'Voice From Above' and quoted from *Humberside Police News* (with permission) it recounts the story of PC Roy Watson from Beverley.

PC Roy Watson, the Beverley GP car driver was returning from an enquiry in Hull, early one evening, when he noticed some young children, obviously bent on mischief. The kids were climbing up onto the roof of a church on the corner of Spring Bank and Park Street in Hull. One of the boys was passing a big stick up to the other children already on the roof.

Fearing possible damage to the church windows, PC Watson drove up to the side of the building. He switched on the car's public address and, addressing the culprits, boomed 'Get off the church roof.'

Of one accord, the miscreants gazed, startled, towards the heavens, scanning the skies with anxious glances. They then slid down and fled panic stricken along the street, totally ignoring the presence of the parked police car.

One can only assume that the threat of divine retribution is still a force to be reckoned with.

Having changed the format of the magazine only five years before, the team, faced with rising costs, decided that from February 1979 the format would once again change, this time to newspaper style. They hoped that the new design would be more acceptable to the casual reader.

James Anderton

One headline that would have attracted the readers' attention appeared in the May 1979 edition – 'New President for CPA'. On his appointment in 1974, Sir David McNee had committed himself to the office for a period of three years. Having now served the Association for nearly five years, he felt that it was time to resign from that post, although he would still continue to support the work. In his place, Mr C James Anderton, the Chief Constable of Greater Manchester, was appointed. Jim Anderton had joined the former Manchester City Police in 1953 following a period of National Service, and was linked at that time to the Manchester and Salford Branch of the CPA. He had also served in the Cheshire Constabulary and the former Leicester and Rutland Constabulary, where he strengthened his bonds with the Association.

Gordon A'Court

In another change, it was announced that Inspector Jim Green (Metropolitan) was handing over the role of Chairman of Council to Sergeant Gordon A'Court (South Wales). Gordon had joined the Cardiff City Police following National Service and had been one of the founder members of the Cardiff Branch of the CPA when it was inaugurated in 1959. He had been elected vice-chairman of the CPA Council in 1968. That position had been passed to Inspector Peter Barnes (Norfolk).

That same year saw yet another tragedy in Northern Ireland. In an article headed 'The Call to Northern Ireland', Peter Barnes wrote,

> On the night of Sunday 3 June 1979 the security forces in Northern Ireland had been called to a community centre near the border at Crossmaglen to search the area after a tip-off that a hijacked vehicle and explosives were in the area. At 11pm after a fruitless search, the police were being 'stood down' when an explosive device laid by the terrorists blew Superintendent Stanley Hanna and Constable Kevin Thompson to pieces. Kevin Thompson was 22 years of age, engaged to be married and a member of CPA. I had been granted two days' annual leave and permission to wear the uniform of the Norfolk Constabulary in order to attend the funeral of both officers. The funeral of Kevin Thompson was held in Portrush and I was able to speak with Charlotte, his fiancée, whose faith and trust in the Lord shone out, even in that dark hour. Mr Thompson, like his son Kevin, had been brought to a personal salvation through the

ministry of CPA. With not having to return to England until the Thursday night, I was able to visit police officers who had suffered at the hands of the terrorists, and also meet many Christian and non-Christian police officers.

As that tragedy evolved, so another was averted in the early hours of Good Friday. Sergeant Terry Lawton (Metropolitan) had been on duty at Tower Bridge Police Station when it was reported that a man had climbed up on to the bridge and was threatening to jump off. Terry attended the scene and climbed on to the bridge himself. While both men clung precariously to the structure, the would-be suicide claimed to Terry that nobody cared about him. In a long conversion with the man, Terry recognised the poignancy of the day and explained how Jesus loved him and had died for him on that day nearly 2,000 years ago. The man eventually agreed to come down – a life saved.

Sadly though, there was more news that affected the CPA central staffing. In April, Harold Wiles, who had been acting as administrator in a voluntary capacity, had passed away. In August the same year, magazine editor Graham Pickhaver announced that he would be handing over the role to Humberside's Detective Inspector Tony Walton, who had been sub-editor and had made regular contributions in *OOD*.

It is perhaps apt, therefore, that in his first issue of the magazine as editor, Tony should include an article with a Humberside flavour. Under the heading 'Radio Stan' he wrote,

The voice of Sergeant Stan Wright is well known in Humberside. His colleagues hear him giving both directions and advice over the radio from the Force Operations Room. The general public also hear him on BBC Radio Humberside when from the Operations Room he broadcasts road and weather reports. But not only do members of the public hear him as a police officer, for he is a regular broadcaster on the local radio channel when he gives directions and advice of a different kind. On these occasions, he may be heard leading 'Morning Prayers' or 'Thought for the Day'. Stan is a founder member of the Humberside Branch of CPA and until recently was its Branch Secretary.

Giving directions is often the domain of senior officers, and perhaps from time to time they need a little guidance themselves. So in the September magazine a 'tongue-in-cheek' senior officer's prayer was offered:

Lord, thou knowest better than I know myself that I am growing older, and will some day be old.

Keep me from getting talkative, and particularly from the fatal habit of thinking I must say something on every case subject and on every occasion.

Release me from craving to try and straighten out everybody's affairs. Keep my mind free from the recital of endless details – give me wings to get to the point.

I ask for grace enough to listen to the tales of others' captures, help me to endure them with patience.

But seal my lips on my own jobs – for the love of rehearsing them is becoming sweeter as the years go by.

Teach me the glorious lesson that occasionally it is possible that I may be mistaken.

Keep me reasonably sweet; I do not want to be a genius – some of them are so hard to live with – but a sour old superintendent is one of the crowning works of the devil.

Make me thoughtful, but not moody; helpful, but not bossy. With my vast store of wisdom it seems a pity not to use it all – but thou knowest, Lord, that I want a few friends at the end.

There were many senior officers who may well have uttered prayers for help the following year. Hostage situations are not regular occurrences in the UK, and most are resolved through mediation before the media are even aware of them. But in 1981 an incident occurred which was to ensure that for a whole week the full force of the media was focused on one particular kidnap. On 30 April, six armed men stormed the Iranian Embassy in London and took twenty-six people hostage. Two things stand out in this. Firstly, among the hostages was a police officer who had been guarding the embassy and secondly, it was brought to a close on 5 May when the Government ordered SAS troops to resolve the situation. The majority of the hostages were rescued, including the police officer, PC Trevor Lock of the Diplomatic Protection Group. The incident set a precedent whereby the Prime Minister decreed that British law should apply to the embassy, despite the Vienna Convention under which the embassy was considered foreign soil.

The hostage-takers and the cause were largely forgotten within a short space of time as Iran and Iraq entered into armed conflict in August 1980. As far as the British public were concerned, many of them would have shown more concern over the shooting on 8 December of former Beatle, John Lennon!

Within the CPA, quite a lot took place during the year. On 1 January, Stanley Wright took up duties as assistant general secretary. Stan had served as a police officer for twenty-six and a half years, leaving the Service earlier than anticipated in order to serve God, working for the Association. He was also a former secretary of the Humberside Branch.

Stan Wright

Also at the beginning of the year, changes were made to the administration of the CPA. Up to that time, the members of the Council had been meeting together with the branch secretaries, but it was decided that the two groups should now meet separately. The Council would have the general oversight of the Association and make policy decisions, while the branch secretaries would look after branch affairs and outreach. The new group would be called the Branch Secretaries' Standing Conference.

There were celebrations in Croydon, south London, in March 1980 when a new police station was opened by HRH The Prince of Wales. CPA member PC Brian Eales, the longest-serving officer from his division, was one of the guests at the official reception. When presented to Prince Charles, HRH asked Brian if he was now old and bold. Brian informed the Prince that he had joined the Force in 1946, and during his first year he had spent night duty watching snow blowing across the front of Buckingham Palace. Brian joined the Association in 1946 as the result of hearing a police witness team in central London which included CPA Council member PC Ron Perrett. Also present at the reception was London Branch secretary, Don Axcell, who was a traffic officer in the area at that time.

By the end of 1980 there had been quite a focus on the Police Service on the subject of prejudice. The features editor of *OOD* picked up on this and wrote a challenging article with the title: 'How Prejudiced Are You?' Within the article, he quoted a study carried out at the University of California in Berkeley just after the Second World War. Their research on the 'authoritarian personality' is still of interest today to those police officers who have to deal with prejudice in any one of its various forms, be it at a demonstration or a street disturbance. It hurts to be called a 'fascist pig'.

The Berkeley study provided a pen-picture of a person

with an unreasonable prejudice. Such a person is one who tends to see the world divided into the weak and the strong. He is submissive and obedient to those whom he considers his superior, but contemptuous and authoritarian towards those considered inferior. He cannot tolerate ambiguity and tends to hold highly conventional values including, where appropriate, church membership.

Such a theory may explain why one individual is more prejudiced than another, but it does not explain widespread prejudice within a society. Most prejudices stem from a community's implicit rules which set out beliefs, attitudes and behaviours appropriate for the members. The individual in such a society who expresses prejudiced attitudes is most likely conforming to the local social norm. Subtle social rewards and threats can induce an individual to conform.

Therefore Christian police officers must ensure that even their language does not contain reference to minority groups which could be construed as disparaging and which simply serve to reinforce the prejudice.

Police relations with minority groups were probably one of the most vital issues facing the Service of the day. The Christian police officer ought to be in the vanguard of the efforts to improve these relations. Community relations work may attract some officers, but the main thrust must be at the sharp end where ordinary bobbies are faced with difficult problems of policing. The high ideals of the service, that every person ought to be treated the same irrespective of their race, creed, colour or social position, were as important then as when Rowan and Mayne's 'New Police' were formed in 1829. Policing has never been easy, but a police officer motivated by the Spirit of God can show the right approaches in the difficult area of prejudice.

Policing without prejudice was and is very important, but within that must be shown a tolerance that allows people to agree to disagree. While the rights of the individual are important, standing on those rights should not result in trampling on the rights of others.

Meanwhile, the recently formed CPA Centenary Committee had been conducting a wide consultation and had put together a project which they were almost ready to launch in 1981. This would be in the form of an appeal to the Christian public to assist the CPA to:

a) establish a branch of CPA in every force area in this country
b) acquire office premises and engage staff to meet the great opportunities which are ours
c) restore, in practice, our international status.

Having completed his two years as Chairman of Council, Gordon A'Court stepped down and was replaced by Chief Inspector Tom Davison of the Royal Ulster Constabulary. Tom, who had been brought up on a farm a few miles from the village of Carnlough, on the scenic coast of County Antrim, had served for twenty-seven years in the RUC.

Looking to the future was not just the prerogative of the CPA. At a Police Superintendents' Conference during the year, perhaps spurred on by the launch of IBM's first personal computer, two senior officers gave their prediction for policing in the twenty-first century.

- They forecast that personal travel would be achieved by feeding a computer with data on destination, speed and time of arrival. Technology would do the rest. Traffic accidents would be an historical nightmare.
- Personal wealth might be measured by the amount of

leisure a person has because inflation and devaluation would leave few commodities or investments worth guarding and these would be in a vault. Even if there was something to steal, scientific security aids would prevent theft.

- People would work from home by computer and closed circuit television so police would not be needed in the streets. Robots would do the menial and manual tasks. Penalties for miscreants would be either cutting their transport and communication links, thus holding them prisoner in their own accommodation, or as a final penalty, their life support system would be withdrawn.

What no one in the CPA had predicted, though, was the resignation of James Anderton as president a year earlier than anticipated, due to pressure of work. This highlighted the enormous burdens that very senior police officers have to carry, and was a signal call to pray earnestly for them. Trying to look after its staff, the CPA Council had granted George Roberts sabbatical leave at the start of 1982. With his desire to see the international status of the CPA restored, he would be using part of this leave to visit Australia, Tasmania and Hong Kong. It would be at the end of his visit, on the journey home, that he would have the opportunity to meet with members of the Enoch Fellowship in Hong Kong. This was an active group of Christian police officers made up of both national and ex-patriot personnel.

George was warmly received by both Christian officers and other members of the Police Service and during his time in the Antipodes, was able to inaugurate several new branches of the CPA.

At the Council meeting prior to George's sabbatical, they had appointed PC Don Axcell (Metropolitan) as the new vice-chairman of Council, and began to consider a replacement for James Anderton as president. It was with much pleasure that at the Annual Meeting following George's return, they were able to announce the appointment of Commander David RE Bicknell of the Metropolitan Police as the new president. David had served in the police for twenty-eight years, much of that time in the Special Branch. In accepting the appointment he said,

David Bicknell

> Many of you will know that I struggled with the decision to allow my name to be put forward to fill such high office and in accepting I am extremely conscious of human weakness and failure, nevertheless I am comforted by verses of Scripture which tell us that we can do all things through Christ who strengthens us and that we should never be dismayed for our God is with us. It is in this strength that I look forward to working with you all in the coming months and the centenary year.

Pressures are always placed on the Police Service and often increased at times of national or international tension. On 2 April 1982, a group of islands in the South Atlantic Ocean became the focus of attention when Argentinian forces invaded the Falkland Islands, claiming territorial rights over this British dependent territory. Involvement in this conflict, so far from the UK, severely stretched the capabilities of the Armed Forces, but they were ultimately to claim victory. During this time, the police at home had to be extra vigilant against any subversive activities by sympathisers.

Later that year, CPA member and former Glasgow police officer, Douglas Allan, considered the demands on the service and how a Christian officer might react. In response, he wrote the poem 'The Thinner Blue Line'.

It's quarter to twelve, on a dark winter's night
As we sit in the muster room, lights burning bright,
The talk's pretty general, the jokes are coarse,
The smoke-laden air is making me hoarse.

The sergeant comes in with an armful of books,
These tell of the stolen cars, break-ins and crooks,
He calls out our duties, we're soon on the street,
Alone, in the chill of night, walking the beat.

Pulling each padlock, checking each door,
Standing by break-ins, chilled to the core.
Going down a dark lane, my heart gives a leap,
A crumpled-up figure; is he dead or asleep?

He's lying in a doorway, half-choked in his sick,
If I want to save this one, I'll have to be quick.
His stomach gets pumped, his life's on the line,
Tomorrow he'll boast to friends, I had a great time.

Marriage disturbances, fights in the home,
Men who get lost in drink, women who roam.
Quietening down parties that are over the score,
Theft, rape and murder, and very much more.

This, every day in a world full of sin,
Where does the Christian policeman begin?
Begin with your prayer life, use faith to make bold,
Show truth and show love to a world that's grown cold.

Be patient, show mercy, against evil be brave,
Tell all that Jesus still is able to save.

Confident in their faith, a number of CPA members from all parts of the UK put their singing talents to good use, and in celebration of the forthcoming centenary produced a long-playing record titled *With All Your Heart*. The album included items from Inspector Bob Cole (RUC), Inspector Ruth Morrison (Lancashire), Detective Sergeant Gareth John (South Wales), Detective Constable Ben Forde (RUC), and Sergeant Bob Black (Grampian). There was also an item from the Grampian CPA Singers comprising David West, Brian Boyd, Bob Black, Jim Boyd and Ally Ritchie.

The year ended sadly as the 'grand old man' of the ICPA, George Paisley, passed to his eternal rest on 22 December 1982, aged ninety. His contribution had been immense and would be remembered by many for years to come.

Chapter 8

The centenary year arrived, and with it some challenges. John Williamson House at Oadby had been the scene of much blessing and many happy memories over ten years, but there was a need to expand the office space and this could not be done at Mosse Way. The Finance Committee had been entrusted with this project and on 6 January 1983, the CPA headquarters relocated to 400 Uppingham Road, Leicester, retaining the name 'John Williamson House'.

On that same day, the RUC's Sergeant Eric Brown and Constable Brian Quinn approached a suspicious car outside a post office in Rostrevor, County Down. There they were shot dead by members of the IRA. Eric, a CPA member, was very much a realist. He was aware that the demands of duty meant walking with death. On a number of occasions he was involved in the aftermath of atrocities, and he was well aware that a violent death at the hands of evil men was always a possibility. He was able to face that reality because he had encountered eternal reality.

After three years in the role of assistant general secretary, Stan Wright had received a call from the leaders of his church to become their pastor. Feeling this to be a call from God, with understandable sadness, Stan felt it right to lay down his administrative post. Determined not to break his links with the CPA it was very much a 'farewell but not goodbye'.

In a shift of focus, the Council felt that the administrative work should be carried out at one location and therefore Richard (Rick) Saunders was brought in as office administrator. Originally from Kent, Rick was living in Oadby at that time.

Finally, on Friday, 8 April 1983, the centenary celebrations commenced with two meetings held at the Guildhall in the City of London. The afternoon saw a meeting of praise, testimony, music and ministry – the pattern

City of London Guildhall

of a normal annual gathering – followed by an evening Thanksgiving Service for 100 years of CPA ministry. The Rev Dr Raymond Brown, principal of Spurgeon's College, was the guest speaker and the music and praise was led by the London Emmanuel Choir. CPA president David Bicknell chaired the evening.

Although that was the main day of celebration, the previous evening a centenary dinner had been held in the House of Commons Dining Room. Following the celebration at the Guildhall, two special centenary lectures were given on Saturday, 9 April at Westminster Baptist Church under the title 'What is Truth?' Dr David Cook of Westminster College, Oxford, spoke on 'A Definition of Truth' and London barrister Mr Peter Duckworth on 'The Application of Truth'. With delegates from home and overseas, it was a very special time for all present.

The celebrations however, were marred by concern and sadness. On 6 April, PC Billy Burns, CPA branch secretary of the Avon and Somerset Constabulary, had responded to a call of an armed bank robbery in Bristol. He had been involved in a high speed chase before the robbers' car crashed. As he approached the car, one of the occupants fired a gun at him. The bullet shattered Billy's front teeth, passed through his tongue and lodged in the back of his throat. Knocked unconscious, Billy was fighting for his life. Thankfully,

his life was saved and wounds healed. He was later to publicly forgive his attacker and meet with him. He was subsequently awarded the Queen's Commendation for Brave Conduct.

Having successfully steered the CPA through the centenary celebrations, all were delighted when David Bicknell was awarded the Queen's Police Medal in the Birthday Honours List that year.

As a finale to the celebrations, in October 1983 the Association published a book, *Never Off Duty, Never Alone* (Pearl) written by Elspeth Jackman. It set out to tell something of the history of the Association and contained stories from many members, past and present.

Often stories are passed on by word of mouth before being recorded in print at a later stage. Within the policing environment, interviews, not immediately put into print, were frequently questioned further on, so even though the technology had been available for a number of years, it was not until 1984 that the police started a trial of tape recording of interviews with detained suspects. As the trial was an extended one, it took some years before this became standard practice.

It is true, of course, that some suspects never get to be interviewed and such was a prominent case in 1984. On 17 April there was a demonstration outside the Libyan Embassy in London. There was nothing new about demonstrations, and policing them was a bread-and-butter activity. That was until 10.18am when, from within the embassy, a burst of automatic gunfire was discharged towards the demonstrators. Eleven people were struck, including WPC Yvonne Fletcher, aged twenty-five, who was fatally wounded. As the occupants of the embassy were allowed to leave the country under diplomatic privilege, no one was interviewed for this cowardly attack.

Don Axcell

As we have seen, the preceding decade had produced regular changes in leadership, which continued this year. Juggling the demands of job, family and the CPA is not always easy, but the Association has thrived on a successive host of willing volunteers. Regrettably, Tony Walton had to relinquish the role of editor of *OOD* and this function had been taken back under the wing of George Roberts at the headquarters. Tom Davison, the Chairman of Council, had successfully brought the organisation through another two years and handed over to vice-chairman PC Don Axcell. Don, a Metropolitan police officer for eighteen years, had been a member throughout that time.

There are occasions when the Association is consulted on wider issues which affect the community as a whole. The CPA was approached by the Archbishop of Canterbury's

Commission on Urban Priority Areas and asked to submit a paper. Following consultation with members who had wide experience in this field, a response was made. In it, the Association made the point that in many cases, churches are seen to place emphasis only on services in church rather than on the needs of the community. The need for practical involvement in the locality was crucial and often beyond the physical abilities of a solitary incumbent. The love of God needed to be demonstrated in action, and taught without apology, either being incomplete without the other. Ideally, the Church should be a positive spiritual base from which all members can witness the relevance of the gospel to the whole person. The report, when completed, was published under the title 'Faith in the City'.

Council member and former chairman of the Council, Robin Oake, had made no secret of his faith when he had moved to Manchester on promotion to superintendent. He had been at Moss Side Police Station when the riots had occurred in that area, and had subsequently been promoted again. In 1984 he became an assistant chief constable in the Greater Manchester Police. In the CPA magazine, the article announcing this promotion was headed 'High Flying Robin!' In recognition of the esteem in which he was held within the Association, Robin was invited to become president in 1985. He took over from David Bicknell, who had travelled thousands of miles in support of the Association during his three-year term as president and would continue to serve as a vice-president.

In the year in which Microsoft invented its Windows

program, the CPA took possession of its first computer. Transferring membership records, mailing lists etc began in earnest, with the hope that it would be completed by the end of 1985.

One thing that did take a long time to complete, if it ever was, was the dispute between the National Coal Board and the National Union of Mineworkers, which had boiled over into strike action in various parts of the country. Large numbers of police officers were transported in a variety of vehicles to supply mutual aid to Forces less able to cope. One positive result was that three members of the West Midlands Branch of the CPA were invited by Central Television to appear on their *Contact* programme to engage in discussion with three miners. Two were striking miners and the other was Malcolm Morley, the secretary of the Christian Mineworkers' Fellowship (CMF). The theme of the programme was 'Reconciliation'. The CMF had been formed in 1980 as a direct result of a CPA member speaking at the church of a Christian miner.

Fellowship between Christians from different backgrounds can be very rewarding, and this was certainly the experience of Cyril Ley, formerly a superintendent in Devon & Cornwall Constabulary who, on retirement, had gone on to become Force Training Officer for the Royal Hong Kong Police. Writing a report for *OOD*, he said,

> From this end, God has been so good. There have been so many confirming experiences that he has called us here … Let me confirm George Roberts' experience with the Enoch Christian Fellowship, I was received like a long lost brother, and, although I can only follow a limited amount of Cantonese, they do insist on my attendance at the Tuesday evening fellowship time. There is always an interpreter who slides over beside me. The fellowship has

decided to purchase its own property, and has just settled on a flat in Kowloon.

At the training school there were about three Christians when I arrived, but now God has blessed us with about a dozen meeting fortnightly in my office. They informed me this week, that an evangelistic rally is planned, and prayed for, at the training school for next February. Praise God.

There are some times, though, where there is a conflict of culture that is not easily resolved. In London, there was tension between the police and certain members of the black community, and incidents led to civil disturbances in both Brixton and Tottenham. On the evening of Sunday, 6 October 1985 on the Broadwater Farm Estate in Tottenham the Fire Brigade, who had been called to a block of flats, came under attack, as did the police officers who were dispatched there to assist. Firefighters and police were forced to withdraw but were chased by rioters. PC Keith Blakelock tripped and fell, whereupon he was set upon by the rioters and hacked to death with knives and machetes.

CPA Council chairman, Sergeant Don Axcell had been one of the officers drafted into the area that night and subsequently was able to visit PC Blakelock's widow, Elizabeth. A team of CPA members under the leadership of Chief Inspector Tom Williamson were ushers at the funeral.

Clive Calver, then general director of the Evangelical Alliance in the UK wrote an article for the CPA magazine entitled 'Christians in Crisis'. In it he says:

> When a policeman is hacked to death on the streets of Tottenham by a group of young teenagers, then we must recognise that something has gone wrong. I lived in Tottenham throughout my teenage years, but things were different then …

Two misconceptions seem to be emerging in evangelical circles. The first indicates that life is basically the same as it has always been, only today everything receives more publicity. The second misconception claims that Christians must adopt an either/or mentality. Either taking on board an agenda for social and political change or adopting concerns relating to personal morality in the nation.

At root, I believe these two to be inextricably linked. Concern for personal and moral issues must not be taken in isolation from a commitment to challenge institutional sin within our society (i.e. where existing institutions dehumanise people due to the way they are structured). Nor can we simply gloss over the fact that the world is in a genuine state of crisis. An unhealthy preoccupation with the marketing of an alternative morality, liberally mixed with large doses of occultism and gratuitous violence has undoubtedly infected our society.

However, to claim that this is the only or even the major cause of violent outbursts such as the recent Tottenham tragedy would be totally naïve.

Evangelicals are rightly concerned about trends of this kind. But they must not become the source of an unbalanced commitment which blinds us to more deeply rooted issues within our society. Along with our desire to see moral change we must focus on the spiritual, political and economic factors which all occupy a place in the jigsaw.

Chief police officers have many factors to consider when performing their duties, relating to other agencies, dealing with situations brought about by socio-economic factors, and the like. All these things have to be taken into consideration when officers apply for senior posts, and interviewing panels have to sum up the interviewee to try to gauge if they will come up to the mark. CPA president Robin Oake's appointment as Chief Constable of the Isle of Man at the beginning of 1986 was greeted with delight, although for the Association it would mean that he was not as accessible as when policing on the mainland.

Still on the mainland, the occupant of the role of Chairman of Council changed hands. Inspector David Walls of West Yorkshire Police, who had been the Chairman of the Branch Secretaries' Standing Conference, took over from Don Axcell.

In an effort to update the image of the Association, 1986 saw the introduction of a logo for the CPA. Trying to reflect both the Association and its links to the Police Service, the new logo  consisted of the initials CPA in a large-size Gill Sans Ultra Bold font sitting on top of a checker band pattern underneath which were the words 'Christian Police Association'. It was printed in dark blue on a white background and was welcomed by the membership, soon appearing on all publications and stationery.

There are some who, by circumstances, are unable to pursue the original course that they thought their lives would take. One such was Godfrey Buxton, a relative of CPA founder Catherine Gurney. Attaining the rank of captain in the First World War, he was wounded four times in twenty-four hours in battle in April 1918 and was awarded the Military Cross and Bar. He was invalided out of the Army and had to walk with two sticks for the rest of his life. His father, the Rev Barclay Buxton had co-founded the Japan Evangelical Band and an elder brother, Alfred, had worked for some years in Africa in partnership with CT Studd.

Committing himself to training missionaries for service, he founded the Missionary Training Colony in 1923, based in Upper Norwood. Having a lifelong interest in the work of the Association and other works of Catherine Gurney, he at one time was chairman of the Management Committee of the Police Seaside Convalescent Home at Hove. For many years he was a vice-president of the ICPA and because of the family connections the Police Missionary Union supported the work of James Cuthbertson in Japan in the early part of the twentieth century. A man outstanding in his generation, Godfrey Buxton died, aged ninety-one, on 1 June 1986.

He would have despaired at the increasingly permissive society that was plaguing the latter half of the twentieth century. Facing up to the challenge, Robin Oake wrote an article for *OOD* titled 'Policing Permissively'. In it he said,

> Policing in a permissive society is infinitely more difficult than one which is simply law breaking. In the latter, there are clearly defined areas where policing is legitimate and where police and public (law abiding and non-law abiding) recognise what is lawful and what is not.
>
> In the former one is talking about morality, which is a dangerous area! We talk today about new morality, which is in effect the old immorality. We are conscious of a lack of integrity, of permissiveness, promiscuousness, a lowering of standards between right and wrong, of harsh jealousies, pride, etc.
>
> Of course, violence and dispute are the order of the day, and in addition, at the social end abuse of alcohol, sex and drugs is becoming more and more common. One has to recognise that the question of policing in a permissive society is one which is over and above law keeping and law enforcement.

In concluding the article, Robin says,

> I suggest in this modern day when permissiveness is the rule outside of the law, and when law itself is abused

and woolly so that its edges are blurred, then we need to make a stand. This is part of the aim of the Christian Police Association that we stand for righteousness. May God enable us in His ability, and with His authority to be thoroughly kitted up in our armour to live in His power to His glory amongst the colleagues and communities where we are placed.

Closely linked to this was an article headed 'Salt of the Earth – Light to the World' written by long-time CPA member John Jamieson, Deputy Commissioner of New Zealand Police. He had attended the Senior Command Course at Bramshill, Hampshire in 1983, had been present for the CPA centenary celebrations in London, and had also had opportunity to visit some branch meetings. In *OOD* he wrote,

> Each new position in the Police Service brings fresh opportunities and challenges, both professionally and in Christian testimony and commitment. The aim of achieving excellence in police service to the community is consistent with Christian goals as disciples of Christ.
>
> One of the most obvious challenges facing us in New Zealand is the constant erosion of standards in many facets of society. The breakdown in discipline, family structure, moral and ethical values together with emphasis on rights without a corresponding consideration of responsibilities has created a vacuum in the lives of young people which is not being filled by humanistic ideas or self- indulgence sometimes justified by liberal or existential philosophers.
>
> Christians are not called to accept deterioration as inevitable. In Matthew 5 verses 13 to 14, Jesus calls his followers to be 'the salt of the earth and the light to the world'. Our effectiveness against corruption is to be seen in the world and not merely in the church.

Wind of change was once again sweeping through the CPA headquarters, and at the beginning of 1987, Rick Saunders gave notice that he intended to leave the Association at the end of July. The Council greatly appreciated his thoughtfulness as it gave them time to plan future staffing. Thus it was that Harry Spain joined the Association that year in the role of assistant general secretary.

Harry moved to Leicester with his wife, Josephine, and their two children. He had been brought up in south-east London and come to faith when he attended a Billy Graham relay meeting. He later met George and Anna Roberts when at the Princess Louise Institute in Deptford. Having trained for ministry at the Faith

Harry Spain

Mission College, he worked with the mission until coming to the CPA.

Among others called to work with police officers was Lionel Ball, a London City Missionary. As part of his duties, he acted as chaplain to the City of London Police and had access to officers at the highest level. He had been carrying out this ministry for nearly twenty years when, in 1988, at a special ceremony, in the Guildhall, Lionel was made a Freeman of the City of London. One of the privileges of Freeman of the City is that they are allowed to drive sheep across London Bridge without having to pay! There is no record of Lionel exercising this right, but he certainly exercised a lot of spiritual shepherding within the City of London Police.

That year was also a landmark for the Police Seaside Home at Hove, Sussex. Having occupied three different properties in the area since 1890, the needs had become much greater than were being provided for. After much discussion

Flint House

and debate, the Management Committee decided it was time to take a different approach to the work, and also move away from the coast. Given that officers were eligible to attend from Forces as far north as Staffordshire, as far east as Norfolk and as far west as Devon & Cornwall and Dyfed Powys, it made a lot of sense to move to a location that was easily accessible to all. And so it was that on 2 June 1988, Flint House, Goring-on-Thames, Oxfordshire was officially opened by Her Majesty Queen Elizabeth, the Queen Mother. With a new title to match the new facilities, it would now be known as the Police Rehabilitation Centre. Physiotherapy, hydrotherapy, stress counselling and general nursing would all be provided, as well as health education.

One person who would have benefited from these new facilities was George Roberts. During 1988, he had spent a number of periods in hospital but, not being a police officer, he was ineligible to benefit from the service at Flint House. By the end of the year, George had written an open letter to members in which he said,

> On embarking upon my leadership role within CPA, Anna and I were totally convinced that the Lord has ordered our circumstances, had established our contacts and had worked in the hearts and minds of the leadership at that time to bring about a clear call to the work of the Association. In spite of difficulties, disappointment and many other pressures there has never been a moment of doubt regarding our calling. Since May of last year my doctor has been urging me to think seriously of my state of health. I have spent three periods in hospital since

October and all that we have gone through since then has underscored the clear leading of the Lord to relinquish office. I want to assure members and associates that their prayers and support have been a great strength to us. My earnest appeal is that you extend the same support to my successor whoever he may be.

Given his frailty, it was something of a miracle, and certainly an answer to prayer, that George was able to be present in person at two farewell meetings for him and Anna on Saturday, 11 February 1989. A combined total of around 600 people attended the meetings to give thanks to God for George's ministry. This was the end of another era for the CPA; a time to look back with gratitude but also to look forward to see where God would lead the Association next.

By the time of the National Assembly (formerly the Annual Meeting) in 1989, the Council had conducted interviews and, after prayer, had appointed Harry Spain as the new general secretary. Responding to his appointment, Harry said,

My wife, Jo, and I are deeply grateful for the trust the Council have put in us. It will be no easy task to follow on from George and Anna. We are conscious of the great heritage of CPA that we have and value your prayers, support and encouragement in the days ahead. I was converted through a Billy Graham Relay from Glasgow to London in 1955. For seven years I was involved with a Mission Hall working through Boys' Brigade, Life Boys, Sunday School teacher and young people's fellowship. It was at this time I met George and Anna, who came to be Superintendent of the Mission. I went to Bible College in Edinburgh with the Faith Mission, spending a number of years in village missions and young people's work. After marriage to Jo we spent the remainder of our time as District Superintendents in that work. Seven years in East Anglia, five years in the east of Scotland and five years in the south of Scotland. At the end of 25 and 19 years respectively Jo and I responded to an invitation to come to CPA to assist the General Secretary, in August 1987. We are far from perfect and are not the same as George and Anna but we do love the Lord and want to please him in our work and witness.

Paula Morris was appointed as secretary to Harry Spain. She would shoulder some of the very substantial amount of paperwork that was involved in running the Association. Originally from Nottingham, Paula had moved to Leicester via Liverpool. She would prove to be a valuable asset to the CPA. Her personal story was told in *OOD* that year, outlining how she had come to faith and her subsequent battle with cancer. She said, 'I spoke quietly to God, "God, I can't handle this." From that moment my thoughts and my life have been very positive. Throughout the radiotherapy, although the effects of chemotherapy were unpleasant, my attitude remained the same. In my spirit, I was at peace and able to come to terms with death itself.'

On the weekend of the National Assembly, news came through of the terrible tragedy at the Hillsborough Stadium in Sheffield when football fans trying to get into the ground were crushed. The disaster was to claim ninety-six lives, with a further 766 others being injured. This, of course, took no account of countless numbers who would be traumatised by the event. As on any such occasion, there had to be someone to blame and the Taylor Report was to conclude that 'the main reason for the disaster was the failure of police control'. However, there were many police officers on duty that day who would carry the mental scars for the rest of their lives as they contemplated their feelings of helplessness as the situation developed around them, seemingly unstoppable.

Chapter 9

A new year and a new decade saw the CPA National Assembly in Northern Ireland for the first time. In spite of the continuing terrorist activity in the province, over 100 delegates from England, Scotland and Wales made the journey to Portadown to join with their Royal Ulster Constabulary colleagues. It was a resounding success on every front, and not a hint of trouble from dissidents.

Neither was there any animosity when the English travelled north for the Northern Branch anniversary, held at Culloden Academy, not far from the scene of the battle fought in 1746. Celebrating their tenth anniversary as a branch, a book entitled *Force for Christ* (Christian Focus Publications Ltd, 1990) had been produced which documented the previous nine anniversaries, recording them for posterity.

Crossing national borders within the UK poses no problems for CPA members, but crossing from country to country in other parts of the world can be more difficult. Former Devon & Cornwall CPA member Cyril Ley, now Force Training Officer for the Royal Hong Kong Police, was sharing fellowship with Christians in that Force who belonged to the Enoch Christian Fellowship. In 1990, a group of thirty-two Korean police chaplains arrived in Hong Kong to visit the police training school. While there, they were addressed by Chief Inspector Patrick Kung, the chairman of Enoch Christian Fellowship, and also by Cyril Ley.

The spirit of compassion that moves many to acts of great kindness can often be found in police officers. These are often reported as 'good news' stories in local press coverage, but seldom make the national media.

With the fall of communism in Romania in 1989, the full extent of human need in that country became apparent. Many organisations were set up to address this, and aid convoys set out from various European countries. On Friday, 22 June 1990, CPA member John Marshall from Lincolnshire set off with five colleagues and a senior childcare officer for their long 2,000-mile journey across seven countries and two time zones, with temperatures reaching 90°F. Their two lorries, a van and trailer were loaded with beds, medical equipment, drugs, food, toys, soap, clothing etc, all donated as the result of a country-wide appeal.

For the police in the UK, the temperature was the least of their problems. There had been a large increase in the number of offences involving firearms, and Forces had to determine the best method of dealing with this threat. Waiting while authorised firearms officers attend a police station to pick up their guns and then attending the incident was no longer the best option, so it was announced that Essex, Kent and Staffordshire Constabularies would introduce armed response vehicles, following the lead of some of the larger Forces.

Following a lead can be a good or a bad thing, and during 1990 the Council had been deliberating on the future of the Association. In his Annual Report of 1991, Harry Spain set out 'Goals for the Nineties', a set of five targets aimed at moving the CPA forward.

- Prayer – setting specific times when branch members and friends could meet together for prayer.
- Regional relationships – encouraging inter-branch fellowship which would be especially important during transitional times.
- Mini teaching conferences – to enable members and friends to share in the type of conference normally experienced only by the leaders.
- Increasing HQ staff – due to illness and early retirement, staffing levels had dropped and needed to be reinstated.
- Increase production and circulation of *On and Off Duty* – with increased production costs, there had been a reduction in the number of issues produced and this needed to be addressed.

The phrase to 'bite the bullet' has been in use for almost a century. It is widely interpreted as to endure a painful or otherwise unpleasant situation that is seen as unavoidable. This was certainly the case for the CPA in 1991. The Association's treasurer, Alan Harris, commented at the time, 'Our financial position can be summed up in one word, precarious ... only about 8% of the membership support the Association in any regular way ... staff and resources are already overstretched.'

As a result, apart from an Annual Report issue, *OOD* ceased publication for a while. It was replaced by a broadsheet called *Extra Duty* which was edited by Sergeant Don Axcell, who was also Chairman of Council.

While things were struggling in the UK, outreach to police colleagues in other parts of the world were doing very well. In Indonesia, there was news of Christian police officers wanting to form their own organisation. In a united Germany, the *Christliche Polizei Vereinigung* (CPV) had appointed a full-time worker and were looking forward to reaching their new colleagues in the former East Germany. In New South Wales, Australia, a number of CPA members found that when talking to colleagues or others, they didn't have the time to explain what Christ meant to them, so they were preparing cassette tapes that could be handed out as and when necessary. In Spain, the Christian police group had been able to place about 4,000 New Testaments in different police stations.

The theme for the Leaders' Conference that year was 'Revival'. This was something that the Association desperately needed in order to capture a vision for the future. Those present felt that they had started a conference depending on their own capabilities, but had finished depending on God. New levels of commitment were made and a sense of direction given. All this in spite of the fact that the husband and wife who were to be the main speakers had to cancel due to illness. This was compounded when Harry Spain, who had stepped in to cover the vacant sessions, was himself taken by ambulance to hospital on the final morning of the conference. These new vacant sessions were filled by the president, Ian McDonald and Don Axcell. A comment from one seasoned delegate was that he had never been to a conference like that before, and that it must surely be the beginning of new things for the CPA.

But more health issues were to hit the headquarters' staff when in December 1991 the office secretary, Paula Morris, was taken ill and it was subsequently discovered that cancer had re-emerged, this time in her liver. Although the worst was expected, those who visited her were aware of a real sense of the presence of God and of Paula's inner strength. To visit her was not so much to comfort but to be comforted. Paula found her eternal rest when she died on Sunday, 5 April 1992.

The previous year, Ian McDonald had taken over as president from Robin Oake. At that time Ian was a superintendent in Sussex Police but his earlier police career had been in Staffordshire. On his appointment he wrote, 'I have been involved with CPA almost as long as I have been a Christian ... and my spiritual growth has been closely linked with the Association since that time.'

Ian McDonald

In the 1992 Annual Report, Ian wrote an open letter to the Association in which he expressed his excitement at what he saw God doing in the Police Service. He said '... the service itself has a growing desire for righteousness and the highest professional standards. There has never been a greater need nor a greater opportunity for Christians to live out their faith in the workplace.'

Senior officers who are willing to live out their faith openly often come under intense scrutiny from the media and minority pressure groups. This was very evident after the Los Angeles riots in 1992, which followed the acquittal of four police officers of assault allegations on Rodney King, an African-American. Bob Vernon, the Assistant Chief of the Los Angeles Police Department at that time, was a man who had made no secret of his Christian commitment. Being someone who was much in demand to speak at conferences, many of Bob's talks were recorded and widely distributed. After the riots, spurious allegations were made against him and extracts from recordings were taken out of context and used against him. Not being given proper opportunity to clear his name, he was forced from office at the end of June that year.

Sadly, this was not an isolated incident, and many others have suffered similar miscarriages of justice in the intervening years. The words of the old police caution come to mind: 'You do not have to say anything unless you wish to do so, but what you say may be given in evidence.' When taken out of context, such utterances can have a very damaging result.

That same year saw another staff change at headquarters. Rick Saunders, who had been office administrator since 1983, felt the need to move on. Although the post was left vacant, Gea Champness, who had worked as part-time secretary to George Roberts, returned to work as secretary to Harry Spain.

It had long been acknowledged that the general secretary could not do everything and be everywhere at the one time. To try to address this situation, in at least one area, the Scottish Branch secretaries suggested that a field worker be appointed for Scotland. With the agreement of the Council, a pilot scheme was set up where Stan Wright, then living in the area, would endeavour to encourage the membership in that part of the country and promote the work, especially where there was currently no branch activity.

Commitment to the task of policing is something that is shared by the vast majority of officers, and the uniqueness of the role has been recognised by successive Governments. But when Home Secretary Kenneth Clarke announced to the Police Federation Conference that he was setting up an Inquiry into pay and conditions, the Federation feared the worst. Sir Patrick Sheehy, chairman of British-American Tobacco, was chosen to lead the Inquiry. There were many who criticised his appointment, particularly from within the Police Service. Fears were borne out when, in his report, he made it clear that the Inquiry did not consider policing to be a unique occupation. Among the recommendations were that an officer should not be eligible for a full pension until completion of forty years' service, the abolition of housing allowance and a reduction in police numbers. John Over, then Chief Constable of Gwent, commented that in thirty years' service he could not recall anything creating such uncertainty among the police. To the relief of the Federation, a new Home Secretary, Michael Howard, rejected the vast majority of the report's recommendations.

While commitment to the task of policing is one thing, openly declaring one's faith can be quite another, and identifying with the CPA yet another. Ian McDonald recognised this when he posed the question, 'What Can CPA Do For Me?' In answering his own question he said,

> God has placed us in the Police Service in order to be his witnesses. The CPA offers all Christians in the Police Service a channel through which they can fulfil their calling. More than that, it provides a support and a wider vision of what the Lord is doing in the Police Service throughout the United Kingdom, and indeed throughout the world. The question, therefore, should not be 'What can CPA do for me?' but, 'What can I do in CPA?'

The task of managing the office and the pastoral concerns of the branches was never going to be easy. If you add into that mix enquiries from individual officers and Christian police groups in other parts of the world, it almost becomes impossible. There had previously been a sub-committee of the Council to oversee

CPA outreach in Europe, but demands were pressing and it was felt that the sub-committee should be strengthened and widen its remit to encompass all overseas work.

So was born the Federation of Christian Police Fellowships (FCPF). With an aim to encourage links with likeminded groups around the world, and motivating and enabling the formation of new fellowships, a network was established that would pool and share knowledge and best practice in creating and maintaining Christian Police Fellowships. Enthusiasm and urgency abounded within the FCPF and it wasn't long before they were planning the first-ever International Christian Police Conference to be held in the UK. With the Channel Tunnel opening in 1994, it was even felt that some delegates might use this means to shorten their journey times.

There was more good news to come in 1994. Following his heart attack in January, Harry Spain was slowly recovering and had been able to get back to work, albeit with limitations. Also, two members had been promoted to very senior ranks. In London, Detective Chief Superintendent Tom Williamson was promoted to commander. Ian McDonald had also been promoted and would become Assistant Chief Constable (Operations) in the Leicestershire Constabulary.

If 1994 was eventful for the CPA with new things on the horizon, the following year was one of headlines for both the Association and on the world stage. On 20 March 1995 a terrorist group unleashed a poison gas attack on the Tokyo subway at the peak of the morning rush hour. This multifaceted attack by sarin gas resulted in a number of fatalities and several thousand people were injured to a greater or lesser degree.

Less than a month later, the largest criminal investigation in American history was triggered on 19 April when a truck loaded with explosives was detonated outside a Federal building in Oklahoma City. The bomb killed 168 people and injured nearly 700. Both these events were committed by citizens of their respective countries and the perpetrators were eventually brought to justice.

Technology was increasingly being used in the fight against crime and the police in the UK had been given power under legislation to collect DNA samples. This also led to the world's first national criminal DNA collection being set up in April 1995, administered by the Forensic Science Service. This would be a huge step forward in the positive identification of suspects in both current and historic cases.

The CPA had endeavoured to keep pace with technological progress by computerising some of the office functions, but 1995 was the year that they would look again at their staffing. In examining the role of the general secretary, it was felt that this title did not really reflect the job that was being done, and it was renamed 'executive director'.

Along with the change in title, it was decided by the Council that staffing levels needed to be augmented and in a copy of *Extra Duty* published in June 1995, an advertisement appeared for the appointment of a full-time assistant director to assist in developing the work of the Association and supporting branches. The Council had felt that even with all the progress in the previous twenty years, the Association was still only scratching the surface and that the potential was enormous.

As applications were processed and interviews arranged, others were making steady progress with the arrangements for the first International Christian Police Conference to be held from 12–15 October at Sunbury Court Conference Centre, a restored eighteenth-century mansion to the west of London and close to the River Thames. Delegates from fifteen different countries had indicated that they would attend, and the main speakers were retired Assistant Chief of Police Bob Vernon from the USA and Chief Constable Robin Oake from the Isle of Man.

The conference was a resounding success, with many wanting to know how long it would be until the next one. The spirit of the conference was, for many, summed up in the words of the song 'Bind Us Together' by Bob Gillman.

While many of the delegates enjoyed an afternoon sightseeing in London, the Council met. One major item dealt with that afternoon was the appointment to the new post of assistant director. Interviews had been held and a recommendation was put before Council. They came to the unanimous decision that Don Axcell should be appointed from April 1996, one month after his retirement from the Police Service following thirty years' service.

Don was a Londoner born and bred. He had always wanted to join the police but, after making a commitment to follow Christ as a teenager, wondered if it was possible to be both a Christian and a police officer. Having become a police cadet, he discovered that there were committed Christians in the Police Service and also there was the Christian Police Association to encourage and support.

Out of training, in 1966, Don got involved with the CPA branch in London and the work of CPA witness teams at weekends, whenever he was available. Out of one such team grew a male voice quartet comprising Joe Neades and Graeme Parkins who were both PCs at Brixton, John Tinnion who was stationed at Carter Street (Walworth) and Don, then based at Tooting. They called themselves 'The Freedom Four'. The London Branch at that time held a monthly meeting in the centre of town and when a vacancy arose, Don became the assistant branch secretary with responsibility for organising the meetings. Subsequently he became the branch secretary and was later invited to become a member of the Council.

After the International Conference had concluded, a number of delegates were invited to a lunchtime meeting the next day at New Scotland Yard. Bob Vernon had mentioned at the conference how he had received invitations to give seminars on ethical leadership in former communist countries in Eastern Europe. The purpose of the meeting was to share further his vision for this work and find out who might like to join him. After the fall of communism, there was a vacuum in leadership ethics and an urgent need to provide training. From this low-key beginning grew what has become the Pointman Leadership Institute.

The following year saw police officers having to deal with an increasing number of terrorist attacks which started with the London Docklands bombing in February, killing two people, and ending, at least on the mainland, in June when a 1,000kg bomb heavily damaged the Arndale Shopping Centre in Manchester where over 200 people were injured.

It was not just the major cities that were to experience the actions of those armed with lethal weapons. On 13 March 1996, Thomas Hamilton walked into Dunblane Primary School in Scotland and shot sixteen children and one teacher dead. The outrage led to legislation effectively banning private ownership of handguns.

In the midst of this carnage in the cities, rural colleagues were having to deal with the outbreak of Bovine Spongiform Encephalopathy, better known as Mad Cow Disease. With travel restrictions in place across the land, many were afraid to venture into the countryside; however, this did not deter the visit of Jim Hammond from the USA. Jim, who was president of the Fellowship of Christian Peace Officers in the USA, arrived in the UK with his wife, Geanie, at the end of May 1996. They were chaperoned around the country by CPA Council member Richard Wiggins and spoke at branch meetings in Hertfordshire and Avon and Somerset.

Police officers in the USA had carried firearms for many years, and there would always be calls for better arming of police in the UK when dramatic gun incidents took place. While such calls were resisted, the Home Office did approve the use of CS gas by Police Forces in England and Wales that same year.

Taking advantage of modern technology was also in the mind of the CPA. In an effort to get the message across, a PowerPoint presentation was put together outlining the work and witness of the Association. It was made available to branches as an OHP presentation, on video cassette or on disk. One attraction of telling the story in this way was that it could be adapted at local level to fit any situation.

Telling stories is an integral part of culture, but alongside that goes the necessity of sifting the good from the bad, the right from the wrong. Equal opportunities and anti-discrimination legislation encouraged more people to tell their stories, particularly grievances, but often a one-sided view was presented. Finding a right way through conflicting accounts is not always easy, and if ever there was a need to pray the 'Serenity Prayer' it was in this situation: 'God grant me the serenity to accept the things I cannot change, courage to change the things I can, and wisdom to know the difference.'

The use of technology in fighting crime has sometimes moved exceedingly slowly, but 1997 saw the introduction of a system that would give Forces a big boost. This was NAFIS, the National Automatic Fingerprint Identification System. This would enable Forces to search for criminals outside their area on a database of over 5 million prints. But however good the technology was, there was sometimes no solution but the dogged groundwork of checking and rechecking in case something had been missed.

There were two events in 1997 that NAFIS would not be able to help with. One shook the world and the other shook the UK. On 31 August it was as if all had come to a standstill on receiving the news that Diana, Princess of Wales, had died as a result of injuries sustained in a car crash in Paris. To this day there are unanswered question surrounding the incident. The other event happened on 24 October, when WPC Nina MacKay of the Metropolitan Police was stabbed to death while trying to arrest a paranoid schizophrenic man. She was the first female officer to die by stabbing in Great Britain.

Isolated attacks like this are thankfully rare, although they do hit the headlines at the time. What often gets pushed down the priority list is coverage of events which are ongoing, such as the breaking of the IRA ceasefire and the return to a vicious cycle of violence. CPA branch secretary for Northern Ireland, David Mitchell, picked this up in his Annual Report but gave thanks that time and time again, Royal Ulster Constabulary officers had emerged unscathed from potentially fatal situations.

One officer who had been left for dead was Inspector Ivan Brown of the Jamaica Police Service. While still young in service, he was attacked by an assailant with a machete and left seriously wounded. Against all the odds he survived, though losing both forearms in the attack. Having been witnessed to by a Christian businessman, Ivan found

Ivan Brown

187

faith in Jesus Christ and his experiences have been widely used to encourage those who face adversity. Ivan was fitted with prostheses and continued to be employed by the Police Service. In 1997 he visited the UK and was able to meet with CPA members from Avon and Somerset and Hampshire Branches.

The nature of the work that police officers are engaged in makes it inevitable that they will face danger, and therefore the support of the public is essential to minimise the risk and assist investigations. Sometimes that support can break down or be lost altogether. When this happens, policing becomes much more difficult.

Following an inquiry into the 1993 killing of black teenager Stephen Lawrence, there was much disquiet among black communities and a general distrust of the Police Service. During this time, the Argentinian-born evangelist Ed Silvoso visited the UK. While addressing a group of London pastors, he challenged them to pray for those who worked in the public sector. Struck by this, one of the pastors present, Ray Djan from Brixton, south London, made contact with his local community police officer, Andy Coles, whom he knew to be a Christian. Together they came up with a scheme to encourage local churches to pray for the police officers who patrolled their locality, and also those at the local police station. This was known as 'Adopt a Cop'. Soon there were more than thirty separate groups praying for their local police on a regular basis. This had a positive impact on police/public relations and a reduction in crime was also

PASTOR RAY DJAN AND PC ANDY COLES PART OF THE 'ADOPT A COP' INITIATIVE

observed. It was time to take this to the rest of the country.

Working with Andy Coles, an information pack was prepared and in March 1998 a campaign was launched in the Christian media. A good number of packs were requested, leading to schemes being set up in various towns and cities. There were, of course, many sceptics within the police who did not believe in the power of prayer, but this was balanced by local commanders acknowledging the positive impact it was having on public relations. One lady later reported, 'Every time I see police officers in the centre of town, I go up to them, tell them which church I am from, how much I appreciate the work they are doing and that I am praying for them. When they pick themselves up, they really seem pleased.'

It was a year that was to see far-reaching changes in the Police Service. The Crime and Disorder Act would require partnerships with local authorities and other agencies to jointly produce a Community Safety Strategy. The MacPherson Inquiry into the death of Stephen Lawrence would make recommendations concerning the conduct of police investigations. The Home Secretary defined goals and objectives for the Police Service and the values by which those duties would be undertaken. The Human Rights Act would also have a far-reaching effect on procedures. Commenting on these changes, Ian MacDonald wrote that branches will have 'a vital role to play in developing Christian responses to these changes and the world in which we live'.

One change that was welcomed by many was the Good Friday Agreement of 1998. It, too, would have far-reaching consequences in Northern Ireland, and many hoped that it would result in a cessation of violence. Speaking on BBC Radio Ulster's Religious affairs programme on Remembrance Sunday that year, branch secretary David Mitchell was asked if his faith ever wavered in the presence of atrocities he had witnessed or had heard about. David responded that we are all human and can lose our faith and the joy of our salvation, but that in his own personal circumstances he had never doubted that God was in overall control of the situation in Northern Ireland.

Part of the vision of the CPA was to have field workers in various regions of the country to build up stronger links between members and branches. The Council were pleased therefore to appoint former Hampshire Branch secretary, Andy Varney to serve in the role for the south-west of England. It was hoped that further appointments could be made in the not too distant future.

Before the end of the year, delegates from twelve countries plus the host nations gathered together at the High Leigh Conference Centre in Hertfordshire for the second International Police Conference. With a millennium theme of 'Pressing Towards the Mark – Christian Policing in the Twenty-first Century' the two main speakers were Mark Kroeker, former Assistant Chief of Police of the LAPD and Robin Oake, Chief Constable of the Isle of Man. Delegates attended from Brazil, Bulgaria, Canada, France, Germany, Hungary, Norway, South Africa, Sweden, Switzerland, Uganda and the USA. A full contingent from England, Scotland, Wales, Northern Ireland and the Isle of Man was also present.

And so we enter the last year of the twentieth century. It seems as if every year in modern history is designated 'the year of ...' something or other. Occasionally they are remembered, but often not. It is perhaps ironic therefore that 1999 was designated the 'International Year of Older Persons' for it is better remembered as the year that

Dr Jack Kevorkian, dubbed in the press as 'Dr Death', was convicted of murder in the USA for administering a lethal injection to a terminally ill man, while in the UK Dr Harold Shipman went on trial and was later convicted of killing fifteen of his elderly patients.

April was a particularly violent month in London with three bombs being detonated and the TV presenter Jill Dando being shot on her doorstep.

For one former criminal, Fred Lemon, 1999 was the year he would meet his Saviour face to face. As mentioned earlier, Fred had a lifetime of crime and confinement behind bars, yet it was while in prison and planning a breakout that he had a real encounter with Christ that changed his life. On release he spent much of the rest of his life making a direct approach to people to make sure that they were 'right with the Lord'. When he first met CPA members he was a little wary of them, remembering a number of unhappy experiences with police officers during his life of crime, but he overcame this and had many opportunities to share a platform with Christian officers.

Facing a journey literally to the other end of the world was CPA honorary treasurer, Alan Harris. Alan was retiring to take up work with a mission on the Falkland Islands. His twenty years' service to the Association was greatly appreciated and he was sorely missed.

As part of the Good Friday Agreement of 1998, the Independent Commission for Policing in Northern Ireland was established under the chairmanship of Conservative Politician Chris Patten. The Commission's report, 'A New Beginning: Policing in Northern Ireland' was published in September 1999. The Patten Report, as it was popularly known, set out to make a number of changes. Principal among these were the renaming of the Royal Ulster

Constabulary, the creation of a Police Ombudsman and a Police Board, the removal of most symbols of Britishness from the Police Service and a new Code of Ethics and Oath of Office.

There was a mixed reaction to the report, with many long-serving and long-suffering members of the RUC feeling a sense of betrayal after years of being stuck in the middle of opposing urban terrorist groups.

After a year of troubles and change, the old millennium bowed out and the new millennium was welcomed in with fireworks and parties around the world. Many Doomsday watchers had predicted the end of the world – it didn't happen. Many Christians prayed, 'How long, Sovereign Lord … until you judge the inhabitants of the earth …?' (Revelation 6:10, NIV UK 2011).

Chapter 10

Although many had argued that the new millennium did not start until 2001, most people celebrated on 1 January 2000. As part of their own celebrations, the London Branch had organised a Prayer and Praise evening for the emergency services early in the New Year. Matt Baggott, then Assistant Chief Constable of West Midlands Police, spoke on the subject 'How to Avoid Those Millennium Millstones' and presented five points: Be believing, Be honest, Be humble, Be open and Be yourself. He concluded with a challenge to all present that 'there has never been a better time to be a Christian. Out there the world is yearning for something. Be different! Make a difference!'

One person making a difference was the new honorary treasurer, Martin Hall. A Yorkshireman by birth, Martin had retired as a senior manager with NatWest bank after thirty-nine years' service. He had experience of the Charity Sector having held treasurerships at the Citizens Advice Bureau and the Prince's Youth Business Trust. His expertise was welcome and would prove invaluable in the coming years.

Continuing its policy of moving the venue around the country, the National Assembly that year was hosted by the Northern Branch at Inverness. Amid splendid scenery, the delegates from across the UK heard reports of the work and were encouraged by the sound of bagpipes to experience the thrill of Scottish Country Dancing. The guest speaker, all the way from California, was Bob Vernon, president of the Pointman Leadership Institute. As the work was growing, more instructors were required and, following the assembly, Bob was heading to the south of England to train a new batch, some of whom had come from as far afield as South Africa.

The Association had always placed great emphasis on prayer and so it was perhaps not surprising that with the new millennium, a new initiative was launched – the National Day of Prayer for the Police Service. In order to get this event into the minds of the churches, it was decided to link the Day of Prayer to a specific occasion in the Christian year. Remembering that, on returning to heaven, Jesus is 'at the right hand of God and … interceding for us' (Romans 8:34, NIV UK 2011), it seemed right to encourage intercession for others on Ascension Day, and thus it was set and became an annual event.

More accustomed to seeing the majestic ascension of a Concorde aeroplane taking off and soaring into the skies, onlookers were horrified on 25 July 2000 to see flames coming from underneath the aircraft as it took off from Charles de Gaulle Airport just outside Paris and shortly afterwards crash, killing all 109 people on board. Every time there is an air disaster, it causes concerns for safety and this must certainly have crossed the minds of some of the 10,000 people from 209 nations and territories who, at that very time, were assembling for Amsterdam 2000, a nine-day conference for preaching evangelists organised by the Billy Graham Evangelistic Association (BGEA), which was due to start on 29 July.

Having previously worked with the BGEA at large events, the CPA were invited to assist in the security arrangements at the conference. Leading the team were Don Axcell from the UK and Byron Hardy from Canada. A number of CPA members also joined the team, including Richard Wiggins (Hertfordshire) and Mark Russell (Merseyside). The event passed without serious incident and all who attended were truly blessed.

The international flavour of 2000 carried on after the Amsterdam conference. In 1998, a young man who had been on mission work in Romania returned to

England and contacted the CPA. He had met some Romanian police officers who wanted to start an Association but did not know how to go about it. After lengthy correspondence, Don agreed to go out there and meet with them at a conference they were organising. So with some trepidation, he travelled to Romania in August 2000 and met with thirty-five Romanian Christian police officers. Before the end of the conference, they had all committed themselves to forming the *Associatia Politisti Crestini* in Romania. They requested further practical and organisational advice from the CPA in the UK and this was joyfully provided.

Hope has been described as 'an optimistic attitude of mind based on an expectation of positive outcomes related to events and circumstances in one's life'.[10] The expectation of great things to come in Romania certainly gave all who attended the conference a huge sense of hope, but in January 2001 another sort of hope was demonstrated among the CPA family in the UK. Former general secretary George Roberts died at the age of seventy. George's faith had been an inspiration to many and this was evidenced at his funeral when Victoria Baptist Church in Eastbourne was packed. A number of CPA members took part in the service and the hymns that were sung expressed the Christian hope of life beyond the grave. This is perhaps best summed up in the last verse of one of those hymns:

> *Face to face – oh blissful moment!*
> *Face to face – to see and know;*
> *Face to face with my Redeemer,*
> *Jesus Christ who loves me so.*[11]

That same sense of family and love was demonstrated in one Force during a night shift. An officer who had been taken unwell had to wait for transport to take him home. Walking into the refreshment area, he found a local CPA member having a meal. In the officer's own words, 'We chatted for a while and I opened up to him, explaining my situation. He listened, gave words of comfort and appeared to genuinely care about the situation I was in. We spoke for about ten minutes whereupon his name was tannoyed to return to the Help Desk. "Do you want to pray?" he asked me. Yes I did, I really felt the need for fellowship, spiritual guidance and strength from our Lord. We spent a few moments in prayer after which he returned to the Help Desk. I was left alone but realised that I wasn't alone. Not only was God with me, but people I feel a bond with and who care for me are also there to listen and help when needed. This one act is what, for me now, the CPA is all about – fellowship.'

Increasing the possibilities for fellowship has always been a priority within the Association, and with the tremendous advances in technology, publications started to become available in Portable Document Format (.pdf).

In 2001, *OOD* was the first to be published electronically in this way. The publications were then able to be downloaded from the CPA website. The opportunities presented by desktop publishing and electronic communication were seemingly endless and certainly led to better and more frequent communication with members and friends.

Communicating what the CPA is about and how it functions was essential if the work was going to go forward. Having trained as instructors with the Pointman Leadership Institute, Council members Paul Bright and Richard Wiggins, together with assistant director Don Axcell, had suggested to the Council that it should set things down in a clear and concise manner identified as 'Principle Based Leadership'. The four-fold advantage of this was that

- it gave the 'why' of what you wanted done
- it gave flexibility – more than one way of doing something
- there is transparency, ie no hidden agenda
- there is responsibility and accountability for everyone.

While this was being presented and discussed at the Leaders' Conference the news was flashed up on television screens that four planes had been hijacked in the USA. It was 11 September and would thereafter be known as 9/11. Two of the planes were flown into the twin towers of the World Trade Center in New York, one was crashed into the Pentagon and the fourth was forcibly crashed due to the actions of passengers trying to overpower the terrorists. At the conference, delegates immediately abandoned their discussions in order to pray.

CPA member Chief Superintendent Neil Wain of Greater Manchester Police had recently been seconded to teach at the John Jay College of Criminal Justice in New  York City on an exchange programme. He recalls seeing smoke rise into the blue morning sky from one of the twin towers and then watching in disbelief as an aircraft crashed into the second tower. Thousands of lives were snuffed out, including hundreds of police officers and firefighters who had bravely entered the buildings in an effort to help others get to safety. Instead of teaching police students, Neil stood with them on cordons, or outside the makeshift mortuary as they recounted their tales and prayed for lost colleagues.

Those events were again remembered at the third International Conference of Christian Police Officers held in Villingen, in the Black Forest region of Germany with about sixty delegates from sixteen different countries.

With the twenty-first century still in its infancy, there would be many events that would make 2002 newsworthy. With the Police Reform Act imminent, CPA president Ian MacDonald hints at this when he writes,

> The police service is once again being asked to undergo substantial changes to its terms and conditions of service. The definition and remit of policing is changing again, bringing the prospect of others exercising powers traditionally given only to Constables. To some observers, it seems a rational and overdue development. To others it appears too radical and destructive to a much cherished institution.

He acknowledged that change can be exciting, but also, at times, frightening. Among the changes proposed were the introduction of Police Community Support Officers and amendments to Anti-social Behaviour and Sex Offender Orders.

In his Annual Report, Harry Spain highlights the demise of the Branch Secretaries' Standing Conference. Once again branch secretaries would meet with the trustees for their Council meetings, allowing for greater fellowship and avoiding duplication of discussions.

It was the year of Queen Elizabeth II's Golden Jubilee celebrations, but before they were able to take place, tragedy hit the Royal Family when, at the end of March, Queen Elizabeth the Queen Mother died at the age of 101. More than 200,000 people over three days filed past her flag-draped coffin as she lay in state in Westminster Hall.

Following the National Conference that year, Ian MacDonald stepped down as president and handed the baton on to Assistant Chief Constable Simon Taylor of Norfolk Constabulary. Simon had a long history with the CPA, having been an active member of the Devon & Cornwall Branch, where he spent the majority of his police service. Writing to members and friends in the magazine, he said,

Simon Taylor

> As Christian police officers and staff we each have a unique contribution to make to wider social reform. Our hunger and vision surely has to be for a world where the light of Christ bombards darkness which might be in the shape of drugs culture, domestic violence, the violation of people's property in burglary or theft or any number of incidents

which front line officers contend with in any week of duty. Part of our calling is to provide that professional policing service which meets the need of victim, investigates well, treats the suspect right and so contributes towards justice. However, the Christian in the job also has another powerful tool. Wherever you go, whatever you do, like it or not, the fragrance of Jesus Christ goes with you. The insight of the Holy Spirit complete with lashings of wisdom, is there to be seized upon – if we ask!

Certainly, a very high standard of policing was evidenced in June that year when the Queen's Golden Jubilee celebrations came to a climax in the UK. The Mall, which leads from Trafalgar Square to Buckingham Palace, became a river of friendly humanity as the final parade joyfully processed, being led by a 5,000-strong gospel choir. It was a great privilege that at the front of that singing throng was the London CPA Branch Good News Choir joining with others in the words of 'He's Got the Whole World in His Hands'.

The following month saw Royal Assent being given to the Police Reform Act, with many decrying its supposed benefits. Lack of manpower and increased paperwork would be some of the complaints and it was noted that while some would make the system work, others would work the system!

As pressure on the police increased, there would be a need for a robust system of support. Matt Baggott, who by now had become the Chief Constable of Leicestershire Constabulary, noted that

Policing can … be a difficult, frustrating and arduous career that can take its toll upon even the strongest individual. It is easy to forget that police officers, and their civilian colleagues, are subject to the same frailties as other human beings. The pastoral care provided by police chaplains is an extremely valuable resource in this regard, both in terms of individual support and also as

a visible demonstration that there is indeed more to life
than 'The Job'.

Matt agreed to become honorary vice-president of the
National Association of Chaplains to the Police, and at the
close of their 2002 conference, one chaplain was quoted as
saying that he thought that Matt had made the most important
statement of the conference when he said, 'The Job is about
changing people, not hitting targets.' It was with that same
sense of the need for pastoral care that assistant director
Don Axcell had been appointed as honorary chaplain to the
Police Rehabilitation Centre at Goring-on-Thames where he
would spend one day a week ministering to both serving and
retired officers who used the facilities there.

If ever support was needed for police officers and their
families, it was in January 2003 when not one, but two police
officers lost their lives while carrying out their duties. On
7 January, PC Ged Walker of Nottinghamshire Police was on
patrol with his dog, Kai, when he went to detain an alleged
car thief. A struggle ensued and Ged was dragged along the
road by the car, sustaining injuries from which he later died.
Just a week later, while carrying out a pre-planned raid on a
house in Greater Manchester, DC Stephen Oake, a Special
Branch officer and son of Robin Oake, was fatally stabbed by
a suspect trying to escape. While their deaths were a week
apart, their funerals were on successive days. On Friday,
24 January, traffic came to a standstill in the City of
Nottingham for Ged's funeral as the procession made its way
through the city, led by mounted officers and dog handlers
to the service in St Barnabas' Cathedral. Although the media
were present in abundance, not one mention was made on
national news. By contrast, the following day, Stephen Oake's
funeral took place in Manchester Cathedral. The traffic was

stopped, there were hundreds of mourners, including the Prime Minister Tony Blair and his wife. On this occasion the national media gave very full coverage. Should it have made a difference? No. Both men were doing a job they loved, to the best of their ability and without thought to their own safety as they laid down their lives in the service of the public. No support can ever be sufficient for such a sacrifice.

Cliff Harries

Following sacrificial service as Chairman of Council since 1996, PC Cliff Harries stepped down on his retirement from the Police Service and handed over to Inspector Paul Bright of Avon and Somerset Police. Maintaining his support for the Association, Cliff had agreed to become a field worker for the Midlands of England, joining Andy Varney (South West England) and Charlie King (Northern Ireland).

It was during 2003 that a new badge was introduced for the CPA. Based on the logo which had been in use for some time, the new design

incorporated a red cross into the letter 'P' of the logo as shown in the illustration.

Meanwhile, support for police colleagues in Romania continued with four CPA members travelling to Bucharest for the national conference of APC with its theme of 'Policing with Certainty'. The conference was held in the People's Palace, built by the former President Nicolae Ceaușescu but which now housed the National Parliament. While waiting to enter the building, Essex Branch leader, Tony Britten, asked the interpreter, Florence Holmes, what it was like to be a missionary in Romania. A smile spread across her face as she answered, 'an opportunity to grow in grace'. Of course, as all of life's problems are faced, they give us an opportunity to react and such reactions will be both observed and commented upon by those around us. The challenge for those who would call themselves Christians is whether or not any such reaction is seen to be worthy of the Saviour they claim to serve and whose grace they have received.

Reaching out to those, as it were, on the other side of the fence can always be a challenge to those in the Police Service who often see very clear lines of demarcation. While some of those lines cannot be crossed, others can. A suspect or offender in custody will have plenty of time to think about their situation, and to try to escape boredom may  request reading material from Custody Staff. Seeing this as both a challenge and an opportunity, Sergeant Julie Parsons of Northamptonshire set about putting together a testimony magazine that told the stories of people who had turned from 'Crime to Christ'. Once produced, Julie gained permission to offer this to those in custody. Should someone then desire to know more about changing their lives, Julie had a network of local church workers who were prepared to offer help and support upon the individual's release. This scheme was also taken up by a number of other Police Forces with backing by the local CPA branch.

A similar work was started in London by CPA member Paul Senior who was concerned at the amount of crime being committed by young people. Aware that this group were unlikely to sit down and read through block text, he worked with illustrator Al Gray to produce comic books which graphically told the stories of those who had found faith in Christ after being involved in violent criminal activity. Several issues of these comics, called *Cops and Robbers*, were produced and thousands distributed. They have since been rebranded *42-Life*.

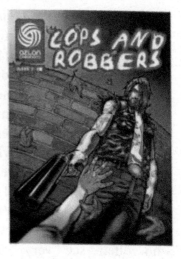

While the CPA had been supporting police officers for over 100 years, there was a new word gaining popularity – diversity. Now was the time for everyone to consider themselves as part of a minority group that needed support and representation, and within the Police Service such bodies were known as Diversity Staff Support Groups (DSSG). Within individual Forces, there would be forums where representatives from each of the DSSGs would meet on a regular basis under the chairmanship of a chief officer.

It was unfortunate that some groups saw this as an opportunity to elevate their cause to the detriment of others and while they called for tolerance, this was the last thing that they offered to others. CPA branch leaders were encouraged to seek support group status, although there was often a lot of explaining to do when it came to the difference between a nominal Christian and one who earnestly followed their faith.

On 24 June 2004, the same day as England were knocked

out of the UEFA Euro 2004 competition, a meeting took place in Committee Room 7 at the House of Commons, organised by a group called 'Clapham Connections' who had historic links to the social reformers such as William Wilberforce. The purpose of the meeting was to bring Christians together in a forum for community transformation. Representing the CPA were London Branch leader, Bob Pull and assistant director, Don Axcell. Discussion took place on how to take things forward and many useful connections were made. Out of that meeting grew the Christian Workplace Forum, which later developed into Transform Work UK, in which the CPA is still actively involved.

It was only just over a week later when the Council met in Leicester. Lying heavily on the agenda was the fact that Harry Spain had indicated his intention to retire on health grounds at the end of the year. After a great deal of discussion, the Council unanimously agreed to elect Don Axcell as the next executive director, taking up his post on 1 January 2005. It was also decided that the premises serving as CPA headquarters and accommodation for the executive director should be sold and the HQ moved to leased office space. A part-time administrator would run the office, relieving that duty from the executive director. It was also decided that no new assistant director should be appointed at that time.

In his farewell message to the Association in the CPA magazine, Harry acknowledged that the CPA was moving on to another phase of its history of work, witness and service to those in the police. He set out the need to always put God first, to strive for God's standard and to be secure in the knowledge of God's ability. There would be much change ahead and many challenges, but as Harry said, 'Put God first, do it God's way, then you can leave Him to supply the need.'

Chapter 11

Having sought the best location for the new headquarters, it was decided to lease an office at Bedford Heights, Brickhill Drive, Bedford which allowed easy access by road and rail. With just 200 square feet of space, it was possible to set up the administrative base and have sufficient room to store various items of stock as well as the CPA archives.

Following contact with a number of churches in the Bedford area, interviews were held to appoint the part-time administrator as had previously been agreed. It was a delight to have Pat Rose from Bromham appointed to the post and she soon settled into the position, mastering the required procedures and technology. It seemed no coincidence

Pat Rose

that Pat had previously worshipped at Brickhill Baptist Church, which was only about a quarter of a mile from the new office. Prior to coming to work for the Association, Pat had wide experience in education and local government. She had also trained as a Christian counsellor.

With one new member of staff joining the team, it was a poignant occasion when, on 22 January 2005, members and friends of the CPA gathered at the Kings Centre, Wigston, to mark the retirement of executive director Harry Spain after seventeen years with the Association. Vice-president Gordon A'Court and Chair of Council Paul Bright made presentations to Harry and his wife, Jo, after which a number of those present gave personal testimony to their faithful service. They would continue to live in Oadby supporting the Leicestershire Branch and maintaining links with the Faith Mission.

The stresses affecting those who work for the police are perhaps no different to those in many other professions, but the rigours of shift work, the unpredictable hours and the dangers faced can all magnify issues within marriage, parenting, debt and work-life balance. To try to address some of these things, the Devon & Cornwall Branch joined with the Care for the Family organisation to set up Family Resource Boards across the Force. These boards held books and videos for colleagues to borrow or acquire free of charge. There was very encouraging feedback from the pilot scheme which covered three police stations, and it was planned to put up another ten boards during the year.

Also seeking the best for colleagues, members of the Metropolitan Branch felt that it was right to give both written and oral evidence to the Morris Inquiry that had been set up to examine professional standards and employment matters in the Metropolitan Police Service. The report of the Inquiry had been published at the end of 2004 and the members of the branch were praying that the Service would take seriously the recommendations of the report.

The professionalism of the Metropolitan Police was soon to be tested to the extreme. On 7 July 2005, four Islamist Extremists travelled to London with terror on their minds. In a short space of time, during the morning rush hour, they exploded four home-made bombs, three on London

Underground trains and the fourth on a double-decker bus. The carnage they caused could hardly have been imagined, as their attacks led to the deaths of fifty-two civilians and a further 700 injured.

The actions of these terrorists would lead to much soul-searching and review of how the emergency services coped with an emergency on four separate fronts. Inevitably there would be change, and the buzz phrase of the year had to be 'fit for purpose'. For better or worse, change would come to both the structure and operation of the Police Service. It would obviously be welcomed by some and resisted by others.

The CPA had to be prepared for change and have the ability to respond to it in a way that maintained effectiveness and support for colleagues. In one respect they were ahead of the game, having looked at a biblical approach to change during the Leaders' Conference of the previous year. One cannot help be reminded of the apocryphal quote of Petronius/Ogburn: 'We trained hard ... but it seemed that every time we were beginning to form up into teams we would be reorganized. I was to learn later in life that we tend to meet any new situation by reorganizing and a wonderful method it can be for creating the illusion of progress while producing confusion, inefficiency and demoralization.'[12]

There are, of course, many ways to transform society apart from terrorism. One person who was passionate about transformation was Debra Green, who had launched the Redeeming Our Communities (ROC) initiative in the north-west of England in 2004. The aim was to reduce violent crime and raise awareness of initiatives which would contribute towards community transformation. One year later it was reported that violent crime in the region had fallen by 11%, which bucked the national trend.

The ROC initiative worked to bring together Christian organisations and churches to showcase best practice. It also provided prayer resources and information to help local groups work together. A special emphasis was placed on praying for the police and the work they do. Chief Constable Matt Baggott, then of Leicestershire, gave the work his full backing and was one of those present at the NEC Arena in Birmingham on 13 May 2006 for the national launch. Around 7,000 people attended the event, including MPs and Peers, chief constables, council leaders and senior Christian leaders. A highlight that evening was when Debra Green invited all those who worked in the police to come to the front of the arena to be acknowledged and prayed for. As many men and women made their way to the platform, there was a spontaneous and prolonged standing ovation by all present in support of the police. It was a very moving experience for everyone. As one assistant chief constable commented, 'It's the first time I have stood in front of such a large crowd without a shield on my arm!'

That same month the CPA vice-president and former Chief Constable of the Isle of Man, Robin Oake was the guest speaker at the Annual Conference of the CPA in Germany. Over 200 people attended and were encouraged to hear of the fulfilment of a project to produce a New Testament for Police Officers in that country, which had taken five years from planning to publication.

In a year which saw the launch of both Twitter and Facebook, it seems hard to believe that loneliness and isolation might be an issue faced by those in the Police Service, and yet there appeared to be a persistent cry during 2006 that 'the job doesn't care about me'. It seemed that the statutory staff associations were no longer able to adequately support their members. In response to this, a plethora of support groups were formed to fill the gap. These were to fit in with the new emphasis on diversity and the Diversity Staff Support Groups. It seemed almost bizarre that in a short space of time the support groups outnumbered the staff associations.

What was worrying in the field of diversity was that some Forces seemed to equate diversity with minority. As a result, those same Forces refused to officially recognise the CPA as a staff support group until much pressure was applied. This situation was slightly ridiculous, given that the Association had been in existence and supporting police officers for many years prior to the staff associations being formed.

The start of 2007 saw encouraging news from the Antipodes where the New Zealand Police acknowledged that the Police Christian Support Network embraced the core values of being responsive to the needs, aspirations and welfare of all police staff. When carrying out a recruiting campaign, they even went so far as to use the story of how a Christian officer used his faith to resolve a difficult work situation. Still in the southern hemisphere, New South Wales CPA member Gary Raymond was congratulated for being awarded the Order of Australia Medal. His citation read 'For service to the community through providing training in the area of critical stress management'.

The Annual Report of the CPA in the UK that year highlighted how some branches were using *Alpha in the Workplace* or *Christianity Explored* courses to reach out to colleagues and explain what Christianity was really about. With so much information available in books and on the internet, it is sad that many are still prepared to criticise or dismiss Christianity without any real cause or justification.

Sadness can come from various causes, and perhaps one of the most frequent is bereavement. Although we rejoice that when Christians come to the end of their lives there is hope beyond the grave, there is still initial sadness which we felt as it was reported that three men who had given much in the service of the CPA were called into the presence of their Saviour in 2007.

On 14 March, George Gladdish, a retired chief inspector who had been the CPA admin secretary in a part-time capacity from 1964 to 1971, had died. On 8 May, Roger Lincoln, a retired chief superintendent who had led the CPA Suffolk Branch died suddenly and unexpectedly at the age of sixty. On 8 August, Doug Hayball, a retired sergeant who had joined the CPA in 1947 and was the founder of the Surrey Branch and subsequently a vice-president of the Association, was called into the presence of God.

As thanks were given for these three men of God, so another great servant was remembered on 15 August at the Northern Police Convalescent and Treatment Centre. Many gathered to celebrate the opening of a rose garden in the grounds of the centre. Within the garden, planted with Gurney roses, was the original headstone from the grave of Catherine Gurney. The Gurney Fund for Police Orphans had commissioned a new headstone, to which the Christian Police Association

contributed. One of the guest speakers, Robin Field Smith, one of Her Majesty's Inspectors of Constabulary, referred in his remarks to the great women of faith who were led to care for those in public service. He said, 'The nurses have Florence Nightingale, the sailors have Aggie Weston and the police have Catherine Gurney – and we must never forget her.'

At the Leaders' Conference in October that year, four new appointments were made. Chief Constable of Leicestershire Matt Baggott was inducted as president of the Association with Assistant Chief Constable of Dorset Adrian Whiting as his deputy. In introducing himself, Matt said, 'In over thirty

Matt Baggott

years of policing, I have found God to be both personal and practical, helping me through both the good and the difficult times with a love that is both constant and true.' Adrian Whiting, in his own introduction said, 'Answering

God's call to be a police officer is never going to be easy – as policing itself is seldom easy – but I am certain that faith equips us with all we need.' At the same conference, Paul Bright, who had retired from the Police Service, stepped down as Chair of Council and Tony Gale was elected to replace him. Dudley Martin was appointed as vice-chair. Before the end of the year it was announced that Matt Baggott was to be made a Commander of the Order of the British Empire (CBE) in the New Year's Honours List.

Tony Gale

The year 2008 was not just famous for the Olympic Games being held in Beijing, nor even the fact that the Church of England Synod voted by a two to one majority to allow the ordination of women bishops. This was the year that the Christian Police Association celebrated its official 125th anniversary. Although Catherine Gurney's work among the police had begun in 1880, it was not until 1883 that the Association was made official.

To celebrate this milestone, a special conference was planned for the autumn. With many international guests, the conference commenced with  a formal dinner at the High Leigh Conference Centre in Hertfordshire. The guest after-dinner speaker was Quintus Smit, president of the CPA in South Africa. The following day a public celebration service took place in All Souls Church, Langham Place, in the centre of London, which was addressed by the Rev Rico Tice, associate minister at the church. During the service, Don Axcell read out a letter of greeting from Her Majesty the Queen. The conference concluded on 2 November with a message from the Rev Dr Derek Tidball, former principal of the London School of Theology.

In an article published in the 1,000[th] issue of the CPA magazine to coincide with the conference, president Matt Baggott wrote, 'One hundred and twenty-five years of the CPA represents a huge legacy of commitment, encouragement and absolute good, not just between Christians but for everyone within the Police Service. I am certain that the next few years will prove to be even more exciting and essential.'

As this narrative draws to a close, the words of that eighteenth-century philosopher Edmund Burke come to mind, 'All that is necessary for the triumph of evil is that good men do nothing.' Yet down the years there have been countless numbers of men and women who have put on the uniform of a police officer with the express desire to do good and influence society for the better. So what more fitting way to close than with four lines from a well-known nineteenth-century hymn, 'Stand Up, Stand Up for Jesus':

> *Let courage rise with danger*
> *and strength to strength oppose*
> *... where duty calls, or danger*
> *be never wanting there.*[13]

And the Work Goes On…

Without the men and women who become members of the CPA and then volunteer their services in various leadership roles around the country, the work could not continue. But continue it has. The end of 2008 was not the end of the Christian Police Association. Branch boundaries correspond to Force boundaries and there is a CPA branch in the majority of UK Police Forces. For this we give thanks to God. There is always more work to be done, progress to embrace and respond to and colleagues to support.

To cover the intervening years up to publication of this book, there is below a brief summary of some of the highlights listed by years. If I have missed something or someone out of the list I trust that you will forgive me, and start the manuscript for the next chapter.

2009 – Former Chair of Council Paul Bright became part-time assistant director, working three days a week. Initially employed for six months, Paul remained in post doing a valuable job until December 2013. Also that year, conscious that police officers often don't have the time to spend in dealing with vulnerable

Paul Bright

people before having to move on to the next incident, some of the Northern Ireland Branch members started the Active Listening Support Team. This consisted of trained volunteers from local churches who could respond quickly and spend much-needed time with those vulnerable people. In September that year, the CPA in South Africa celebrated fifteen years since reforming their group. Paul Bright, Chris Geen (Thames Valley) and Don Axcell represented the CPA in the UK at their conference. This was also the year when Matt Baggott left Leicestershire Police to become Chief Constable of the Police Service of Northern Ireland.

2010 – Thanks in great measure to the work of Paul Bright, the CoAct project was launched to encourage Christians everywhere to be involved in prayerful and practical involvement in their local policing. In May, Paul embarked on a marathon pushbike ride around Britain. Called 'Catch the Vision', Paul rode 1,524 miles in twenty-two days, visiting CPA members in eighteen different Forces. In June, the CPA group in Romania celebrated ten years since their formation with a special conference. September saw Metropolitan Branch member Mike Smith, who had founded the Word 4 Weapons movement, launch their eleventh knife bin in London; he received a Community Engagement Award from the Mayor of London. In October, the Pan African Christian Police Associations Conference held their fifth conference in Nairobi, Kenya at which seventeen countries were represented. Delegates from the UK were Simon Werrett (Essex) and Allan Spencer (Avon and Somerset).

2011 – In April, at the National Conference held in Scotland, administrator Pat Rose retired, and was succeeded by Jackie Gillen. In May, Don Axcell and Dudley Martin joined police officers in the Czech Republic for the inauguration of a CPA work in that country. Sadly, August was marred by riots in London and other major UK cities when police came under attack and there was widespread looting. The end of September saw the first European Conference of Christian Police Officers held in Guadalajara,

Jackie Gillen

Spain. Tony Britten (Essex), Bert Sharp (Scotland) and Don Axcell represented the UK. Volunteer regional coordinators were introduced in the UK to give more support to branch leaders, the first two being Mike Quinnell (North West) and Phil Skedgell (South West).

2012 – By far the biggest event for the CPA was the publication of a Police Pocket Testament in time for the London Olympic Games. The Testament contained relevant material for police officers as well as the whole of the New Testament, the book of Psalms and the book of Proverbs. A good number were distributed to officers employed

at various Olympic venues. The Association embraced the benefits of social media with Facebook and Twitter accounts being incorporated into the CPA website.

2013 – Keen to promote the work of the CPA, pens and mugs with the logo were made available for distribution. The World Police and Fire Games held in Northern Ireland provided a great opportunity to work alongside colleagues from Firefighters for Christ. At the end of the year, Paul Bright retired from his post as assistant director.

2014 – In October, the Word 4 Weapons organisation held a Community Awards ceremony in London. A special award was made to the CPA in recognition of the support given since W4W was formed. At the Leaders' Conference in November, Allan Spencer was appointed to the role of part-time assistant director from 1 January 2015.

Allan Spencer

2015 – In June, CPA administrator Jackie Gillen married Philip White and the ceremony was conducted by Don Axcell. In the autumn it was with sadness that we

recorded the deaths of two long-time servants of the CPA; in September former branch leader and editor of the CPA magazine Tony Walton, followed in October by vice-president and former assistant general secretary Stan Wright. At the Leaders' Conference in November, Lee Russell was appointed to succeed Don Axcell as executive director from 1 May 2016.

Lee Russell

Apart from the **Christian Police Association**, other organisations keeping the vision of Catherine Gurney very much alive in the twenty-first century are the **Police Rehabilitation Centre** at Goring-on-Thames and the **Police Treatment Centres** at Harrogate and Auchterarder. Together, the three centres treat nearly 8,000 serving and retired police officers every year. In addition to this, the **Gurney Fund** in the south and the **St George's Police Children Trust** in the north continue to assist and support the children of police officers, where a parent has died or has had to retire on ill health grounds.

Whether as staff or volunteers, the men and women who maintain the work of these five charities do so from a sense of recognition of the worth of those who guard our streets twenty-four hours a day, 365 days a year. May their work continue to be blessed in the years to come.

Gurney Family Tree

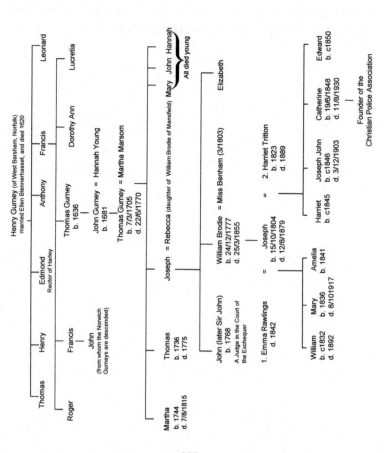

Henry Gurney (of West Barsham, Norfolk)
married Ellen Blennerhasset, and died 1620

Thomas   Henry   Edmond   Anthony   Francis   Leonard
      Rector of Harley

Roger   Francis   Dorothy Ann   Lucretia

John
(from whom the Norwich
Gurneys are descended)

Thomas Gurney
b. 1636

John Gurney = Hannah Young
b. 1681

Thomas Gurney = Martha Marsom
b. 7/3/1705
d. 22/6/1770

Martha
b. 1744
d. 7/8/1815

Thomas
b. 1736
d. 1775

Joseph = Rebecca (daughter of William Brodie of Mansfield)   Mary   John   Hannah
                                              All died young

John (later Sir John)
b. 1768
A Judge in the Court of
the Exchequer

William Brodie = Miss Benham (3/1803)
b. 24/12/1777
d. 25/3/1855

Elizabeth

1. Emma Rawlings
d. 1842

=   Joseph   =
b. 15/10/1804
d. 12/8/1879

2. Harriet Tritton
b. 1823
d. 1889

William
b. c1832
d. 1892

Mary
b. 1836
d. 8/10/1917

Amelia
b. 1841

Harriet
b. c1845

Joseph John
b. c1846
d. 3/12/1903

Catherine
b. 19/6/1848
d. 11/8/1930

Edward
b. c1850

Founder of the
Christian Police Association

Endnotes

Introduction
1   Michael Nila and Stephen Covey, *The Nobility of Policing* (Franklin Quest: November 2008).

Chapter 1
2   Sir Robert Peel, *Principles of Law Enforcement 1829*.

Chapter 2
3   'All Things Bright and Beautiful', CF Alexander, 1818–95. Public Domain.

Chapter 4
4   Tributes recorded in JM Tritton, *A Beloved Lady* (ICPA 1931), pp 43–53.
5   *Police Review* a weekly magazine for the police published between 1893 and 2011. Tribute reproduced in *A Beloved Lady*.
6   JM Tritton, *A Beloved Lady* (quoted on title page) (ICPA, 1931).

Chapter 5
7   'Service, Not Force' in *The Times*, 4 April 1936.

8   *Church of England Newspaper* 15 August 1947, quoted in *OOD* January 1949

Chapter 7
9   'Christmas arrest' © CS Porteous 1972. By kind permission.

Chapter 10

10 Quoted by Rev Margaret Minnicks, Richmond Christian
Education Examiner, in Examiner.com, 19 January 2016

11 'Face to Face with Christ, my Savior', Carrie E Breck, 1855–1934.
Public Domain.

Chapter 11

12 Falsely attributed to Gaius Petronius Arbiter. Quote is from
Charlton Ogburn, Jr. (1911–98), in Harper's Magazine, "Merrill's
Marauders: The truth about an incredible adventure" (Jan 1957).

13 'Stand up, stand up for Jesus', George Duffield, Jr, 1818–88.
Public Domain.